# cakes

This edition published in 2011 by
**CHARTWELL BOOKS, INC.**
A division of BOOK SALES, INC.
276 Fifth Avenue Suite 206
New York, New York 10001
USA

This edition published by arrangement with Flame Tree Publishing,
an imprint of The Foundry Creative Media Company Limited
Crabtree Hall, Crabtree Lane
Fulham, London SW6 6TY
United Kingdom
www.flametreepublishing.com

**Publisher's Note:**
Raw or semicooked eggs should not be consumed by babies, toddlers, pregnant or breast-feeding women,
the elderly, or people with a chronic illness.

**Publisher & Creative Director:** Nick Wells
**Senior Project Editor:** Catherine Taylor
**Editorial:** Laura Bulbeck
**Art Director:** Mike Spender
**Layout Design:** Jane Ashley
**Digital Design & Production:** Chris Herbert
**Proofreader:** Dawn Laker

Special thanks to Charlotte McLean, Digby Smith and Helen Wall.

ISBN-13: 978-0-7858-2864-8

Printed in China

All images © Foundry Arts except the following, which are courtesy of Shutterstock and © the following photographers:
Pamela Uyttendaele 11br; alika 16.

# cakes

Gina Steer

CHARTWELL
BOOKS, INC.

# Contents

# Introduction

Cakes have long been part of celebrations in various forms, as well as being considered delicious treats for more informal times. Home baking offers the opportunity to whip up both easy-to-make cakes and slightly more sophisticated offerings, in various shapes and sizes.

Home-made cakes are cheaper than store-bought cakes, quick and easy to make and provide delicious treats, as well as being great for birthdays, Christmas or other celebrations. There is no comparison to the quality of home-made cakes and the fun to be had in making them. Children love to get involved in baking cakes, which provides a fun and creative family activity. Baking and decorating yourself also means you can personalize them for whatever the occasion and cater for your personal preference. This book has a wide range of recipes, some very quick and easy, some requiring a little more patience.

Another advantage of making your own cakes is that you can control which ingredients you use, thus ensuring that none of the ingredients will trigger any allergies.

This book will show you how easy it is to make and bake cakes and you will find many different varieties to try, from classic layer cakes to loaf cakes and cupcakes. By following the advice from preparation to decoration, you will discover for yourself how rewarding it is to taste and show off a cake you have made yourself!

## Using This Book

This book is aimed at showing both the occasional and well-practiced baker how to create delicious cakes, both for special occasions and simply for an afternoon treat. The recipes in this book are divided into handy categories, covering everyday

good to you. The best idea is to read the recipe through thoroughly and then assemble and measure out all the ingredients you will need. Preheating your oven will also ensure that your cake will cook to its best.

## Measuring

The recipes contained in this book mostly provide cup measurements or other quantities where appropriate. All spoon measurements should be used level for accuracy, and always use a recognized set of spoon measures for best results. Ensuring that the ingredients are accurately measured is vital for baking success, therefore a good set of measuring cups (and perhaps a liquid measuring cup) is very important. Read the ingredients lists carefully—a cake that has too much flour or insufficient egg will be dry and crumbly. Too much leavening agent will mean that the cake will rise too quickly and sink. Insufficient leavening agent means the cake will not rise in the first place.

cakes, chocolate cakes, and special occasion and dessert cakes for when you want to entertain or make something really special. By reading the guide to equipment and ingredients at the front of the book, as well as decoration tips, baking cakes will be made far easier and result in success much more often.

The essential cake baking ingredients are discussed, covering the varying types of fat, flour, eggs and sugar. Basic but important techniques such as how to line cake pans correctly and different methods of mixing are covered, and once mastered will help build your confidence in baking. We then go on to look at the various ways to decorate your cakes, including a section dedicated to handling chocolate.

First read through the advice at the beginning of this book, and then have a go at choosing a recipe which looks

## Using Your Oven

Ensure that the oven is preheated to the correct temperature; it can take 10–15 minutes to reach 350°F. You may find that an oven thermometer is a good investment. Cakes are best if cooked in the center of the preheated oven. Try to avoid opening the oven door at the start of cooking as a draft can make the cake sink. If using a convection oven you will need to reduce the temperature stated in the recipe, and it is best to refer to the manufacturer's instructions. Check that the cake is thoroughly cooked by removing from the oven and inserting a clean skewer. Let stand for 30 seconds and remove. If clean, then the cake is cooked, if there is a little mixture return to the oven for a few minutes.

## Avoiding Problems

When you take your cake out of the oven, unless the recipe states that it should be left in the pan until cold, let stand for a few minutes, then loosen the edges and turn out onto a wire rack to cool. Cakes that are left in the pan for too long, tend to sink or slightly overcook. When storing, make sure the cake is completely cold before placing it into an airtight container.

Other problems encountered during cake making are insufficient creaming of the fat and sugar or a curdled mixture (which will result in a fairly solid cake). Flour that has not been folded in carefully enough or has not been mixed with enough leavening agent may also result in a fairly heavy consistency. Be aware—especially when cooking with fruit—that if the consistency is too soft, the cake will not be able to support the fruit. Ensure that the correct size of pan is used as you may end up either with a flat, hard cake or one which has spilled over the edge of the pan.

# Equipment and Utensils

Cooking equipment not only assists in the kitchen, but can make all the difference between success and failure. Take the humble cake pan, although a very basic piece of cooking equipment, it plays an essential role in baking. Using a pan that is too large will spread the mixture too thinly and the result will be a flat, limp-looking cake. On the other hand, cramming the mixture into a pan which is too small will result in the mixture rising up and out of the pan.

## Bakeware

To ensure successful baking it is worth investing in a selection of high quality pans which, if looked after properly, should last for many years. Follow the manufacturer's instructions when first using and ensure that the pans are thoroughly washed and dried after use and before putting away.

### Sandwich Cake Pans

Perhaps the most useful of pans for baking are sandwich cake pans, ideal for classics such as Victoria sponge cake, Genoese cake and coffee and walnut cake. You will need two pans,

normally 7–8 inches in diameter and 2–3 inches deep and often nonstick.

### Deep Cake Pans

With deep cake pans, it is personal choice whether you buy round or square pans and they vary in size from 5–14 inches with a depth of between 5–6 inches. A deep cake pan, for everyday fruit or Madeira cake is a must, a useful size is 8 inches.

### Loaf Pans

Loaf pans normally come in two sizes, 1 lb. and 2 lb.

## Other Pans

There are plenty of other pans to choose from, ranging from themed and shaped tins, such as Christmas trees, numbers, and petals, to ring mold pans (pans with a hole in the center) and springform tins, where the sides release after cooking, letting the finished cake be removed easily. A selection of different sized roasting pans are also a worthwhile investment as they can double up as a *bain-marie*, or for cooking larger quantities of cakes, such as gingerbread.

## Other Essential Items

### Mixing bowls

Three to four different sizes of mixing bowls are also very useful for mixing and melting ingredients.

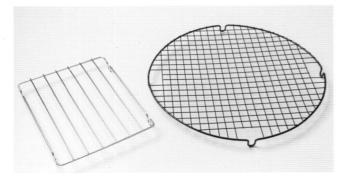

### Wire Cooling Racks

Another essential piece of equipment is a wire rack. It is essential when baking to let cakes cool after being removed from their pans. A wire rack also protects your kitchen surfaces from the heat and allows air to circulate around the goodies, speeding cooling and preventing the base from becoming soggy.

### Measuring Cups and Cutlery

Baking needs 100 percent accuracy to ensure a perfect result. Measuring cups come in sets, using ¼, ⅓, ½, and 1 cup. Make sure you level off the ingredient unless otherwise instructed. Measuring pitchers and spoons are essential for accurate measuring of liquid or small amounts of ingredients. Basic mixing cutlery is also essential such as a wooden spoon (for mixing and creaming), a plastic spatula (for transferring the mixture from the mixing bowl to the baking pans and spreading the mixture once it is in the pans) and a straight-sided spatula (to ease cakes out of their pans before placing them on the wire racks to cool).

## Electrical Equipment

Nowadays help from time-saving gadgets and electrical equipment make baking far easier and quicker. Equipment can be used for creaming, mixing, beating, whisking, grating, and chopping. There is a wide choice of machines available from the most basic to the highly sophisticated.

## Food Processors

First decide what you need your processor to do when choosing a machine. If you are a novice to baking, it may be a waste to start with a machine that offers a wide range of implements and functions. This can be off-putting and result in not using the machine to its ultimate.

When buying a food processor look for measurements on the side of the processor bowl and machines with a removable feed tube, which lets food or liquid be added while the motor is still running. Look out for machines that have the facility to increase the capacity of the bowl and have a pulse button for controlled chopping. For many, storage is an issue so reversible discs and flex storage, or on more advanced models, a blade storage compartment or box, can be advantageous.

It is also worth thinking about machines that offer optional extras, which can be bought as your cooking requirements change. Mini-chopping bowls are available for those wanting to chop small quantities of food. If time is an issue, dishwasher-friendly attachments may be vital. Citrus presses, liquidizers, and whisks may all be useful attachments for the individual cook.

## Blenders

Blenders often come as attachments to food processors and are generally used for liquidizing and puréeing foods. There are two main types of blender. The first is a table-top version. The blades of this blender are at the bottom of the jar with measurements up the sides. The second blender is portable. It is hand-held and should be placed in a bowl to blend.

## Table-Top Mixers

The table-top mixers are freestanding and are capable of dealing with fairly large quantities of mixture. They are robust machines and good for heavy cake mixing as well as whipping cream, whisking egg whites, or making one-stage cakes. These mixers also offer a wide range of attachments ranging from liquidizers, mincers, juicers, can openers, and many more and varied attachments.

## Hand-Held Mixers

Hand-held mixers are smaller than freestanding mixers and often come with their own bowl and stand from which they can be lifted off and used as hand-held devices. They have a motorized head with detachable twin whisks. These mixers are particularly versatile as they do not need a specific bowl in which to whisk. Any suitable mixing bowl can be used.

# Essential Ingredients

The quantities may differ, but basic baking ingredients do not vary greatly. Let us take a closer look at the baking ingredients which are essential.

## Fat

Butter and margarine are the fats most commonly used in baking. Others that can be used include white vegetable fat, lard, and oil. Low-fat spreads are not recommended for baking because they break down when cooked at a high temperature. Often it is a matter of personal preference which fat you choose when baking, but there are a few guidelines that are important to remember.

### Butter and Margarine

Unsalted butter is the fat most commonly used in cake making, especially in rich fruit cakes and the heavier sponge cakes, such as Madeira or chocolate torte. Unsalted butter gives a distinctive flavor to the cake. Some people favor margarine, which imparts little or no flavor to the cake.

As a rule, butter and firm block margarine should not be used straight from the refrigerator, but allowed to come to room temperature before using (allow about an hour to soften). Also, it should be beaten by itself first before creaming or rubbing in. Soft margarine is best suited to one-stage recipes.

## Oil

Light oils, such as vegetable or sunflower, are sometimes used instead of solid fats. However, if oil is used, be careful—it is vital to follow a specific recipe because the proportions of oil to flour and eggs are different and these recipes will need extra leavening agents.

## Flour

We can buy a wide range of flour all designed for specific jobs. There is even a special sponge flour designed specifically for whisked sponges. It is also possible to buy flours that cater for celiacs, which contain no gluten. Buckwheat, soy, and chickpea flours are also available. Flour can also come ready sifted.

## Which Flour to Use

Bread flour, which is rich in gluten, whether it is white or brown (this includes granary and stoneground), is best kept for bread and steamed suet puddings. Ordinary flour is best for cakes, which absorbs the fat easily and give a soft light texture. This flour comes in all-purpose or self-rising, as well as wholewheat. Self-rising flour, which has the leavening agent already incorporated, is best kept for sponge cakes where it is important that an even rise is achieved.

All-purpose flour can be used for all types of baking. If using all-purpose flour for cakes, unless otherwise stated in the recipe, use 1 teaspoon of baking powder to two cups of all-purpose flour. With sponge cakes and light fruit cakes, it is best to use self-rising flour as the leavening agent has already been added to the flour. This way there is no danger of using too much, which can result in a sunken cake with a sour taste.

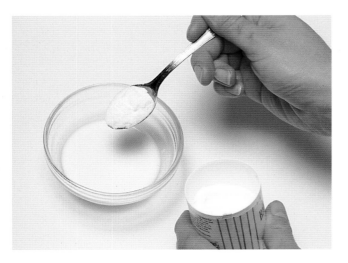

## Other Leavening Agents

There are other leavening agents that are also used. Some cakes use baking soda with or without cream of tartar, blended with warm or sour milk. Whisked eggs also act as a leavening agent as the air trapped in the egg ensures that the mixture rises. Generally no other leavening agent is required.

## Eggs

There are many types of eggs sold and it really is a question of personal preference which ones are chosen. All offer the same nutritional benefits. Store the eggs in the refrigerator with the round end uppermost, and allow to come to room temperature before using.

### Sizes

When a recipe states 1 egg, it is generally accepted that this refers to a large egg (24 oz. per dozen.) Eggs come in a variety of sizes, however, and sometimes when baking, a recipe will state the egg size that should be used. Other eggs sizes available, based on their minimum weight per dozen, are: jumbo (30 oz.), extra large (27 oz.), medium (21 oz.), small (18 oz.), and peewee (15 oz.).

### Types

Whether the shells are brown, white, or even green or blue, all offer the same nutritional benefits. The color of the egg yolk will depend on the diet the hen has been fed on, so wheat-fed hens lay eggs with darker yolks, and feeds of alfalfa, corn, and grass lead to eggs with lighter yolks.

It is commonly thought that free-range eggs are from hens that lead a much more natural life and are fed natural foods. This, however, is not always the case—there are no USDA standards—and, in some instances, they may still live in a crowded environment. Organic eggs are from hens that live in a flock, whose beaks are not clipped, and who are completely free to roam. Obviously, these eggs are much more expensive than the others.

## Safety

Most hens' eggs on the market have been graded according to quality and size under USDA standards. Eggs are graded AA, A, and B, and the classification is determined by interior and exterior quality. Interior quality is judged by "candling," where the eggs roll over high-intensity lights to allow their insides to be examined. The exterior quality of an egg is determined by a number of factors, such as the soundness, cleanliness, shape, and texture of the eggshell. Do remember, raw or semicooked eggs should not be given to babies, toddlers, pregnant women, the elderly, and those suffering from a recurring illness.

# Sugar

Sugar not only offers taste to baking, but also adds texture and volume to the mixture.

## Which Sugar to Use

It is generally accepted that superfine sugar is best for sponge cakes. Its fine granules disperse evenly when creaming or whisking. Granulated sugar is used for more general cooking, such as stewing fruit, whereas raw sugar with its toffee taste and crunchy texture is good for sticky desserts and cakes. For rich fruit cakes, Christmas puddings, and cakes, use the brown sugars, which give a rich intense molasses flavor. Confectioners' sugar is used primarily for frostings and can be used in fruit sauces when the sugar needs to dissolve quickly.

## Flavored Sugar

For a different flavor, try flavoring your own sugar. Place a vanilla pod in a screw-top jar, fill with superfine sugar, screw down the lid and leave for 2–3 weeks before using. Top up after use or use thinly pared lemon or orange rind in the same manner.

## Reducing Sugar Intake

If you are trying to reduce sugar intake, then use the unrefined varieties of granulated sugar (pictured above left), and the brown sugars (raw sugar pictured above right). All of these are a little sweeter than their refined counterparts, so less is required. Alternatively, honey or fructose (fruit sugar) can reduce sugar intake as they have similar calories to sugar, but are twice as sweet. Their effect also lasts longer.

# Working with Chocolate

Chocolate can be used in cakes to create flavor and color, as well as to decorate. Who can resist its charms?

## Melting Chocolate

As a general rule, it is important not to let any water come into contact with the chocolate. In fact, a drop or two of water is more problematic than larger amounts, which may blend in. The melted chocolate will "seize" (turn into a grainy, clumpy mess) and it will be impossible to bring it back to a smooth consistency.

Do not overheat chocolate or melt it by itself in a pan over a direct heat. Always use either a double boiler or a heatproof bowl set over a saucepan of water, but do not let the bottom of the bowl come into contact with the water. Check the chocolate every couple of minutes, reducing or extinguishing the heat under the saucepan, as necessary.

Stir the chocolate once or twice during melting until it is smooth and no lumps remain. Do not cover the bowl once the chocolate has melted or condensation will form, water will drop into it and it will be ruined.

Microwaving is another way of melting chocolate, but again, caution is required. Follow the oven manufacturer's directions together with the directions on the chocolate and proceed with care. Melt the chocolate in intervals of 30–60 seconds, stirring well between intervals until the chocolate is smooth. If possible, stop microwaving before all the chocolate has melted and let the residual heat in the chocolate to finish the job.

## Making Chocolate Decorations

There are a few useful techniques for working with chocolate. None of them are very complicated, and all can be mastered easily with a little practice.

## Curls

To make curls melt the chocolate following your preferred method then spread it in a thin layer over a cool surface, such as a marble slab, ceramic tile or piece of granite. Let stand until just set but not hard. Take a clean paint scraper or cheese plane and set it at an angle to the surface of the chocolate, then push, taking a layer off the surface. This will curl until you release the pressure.

## Thin Curls

To make long thin curls, prepare the chocolate in the same way as for the curls. Use a large sharp knife and hold it at about a 45-degree angle to the chocolate. Hold the handle and the tip and scrape the knife towards you pulling the handle but keeping the tip more or less in the same place. This method makes thinner, tighter, longer curls.

## Shaved and Grated Chocolate

Using a vegetable peeler, shave a thick block of chocolate to make mini-curls or use a sharp long-bladed knife to make big shavings. These are best achieved if the chocolate is a little soft, otherwise it has a tendency to break into little flakes. Or, use a grater to achieve even tinier shavings.

## Chocolate Shapes

Spread a thin layer of chocolate, as described in the instructions for chocolate curls, and let set as before. Use shaped cutters or a sharp knife to cut out shapes. Use to decorate your cakes.

## Modeling Chocolate

To make modeling chocolate (very useful for cake coverings and for making heavier shapes, like ribbons) put 7 oz. unsweetened chocolate in a bowl and add 3 tablespoons of liquid glucose or light corn syrup. Set the bowl over a saucepan of gently simmering water. Stir until the chocolate is just melted then remove from the heat. Beat until smooth and let mixture cool. When cool enough to handle, knead to a smooth paste on a clean work surface. The mixture can now be rolled and cut to shape to make ropes, braids and cake coverings etc. If the paste hardens, wrap it in plastic wrap and warm it in the microwave for a few seconds on low.

# Basic Methods

## Lining

If a recipe states that the pan needs lining do not be tempted to ignore this. Rich fruit cakes and other cakes that take a long time to cook benefit from the pan being lined so that the edges and bottom do not burn or dry out.

### Papers

Waxed paper or parchment paper is ideal for this. It is a good idea to have the paper at least double thickness, or preferably three to four layers. Sponge cakes and other cakes that are cooked in 30 minutes or less are also better if the bottoms are lined as it is far easier to remove them from the pan.

### Technique

The best way to line a round or square pan is to draw lightly around the bottom, then cut just inside the markings, making it easy to sit in the pan. Next, lightly oil the paper so it peels easily away from the cake. If the sides of the pan also need to be lined, then cut a strip of paper long enough for the pan. This can be measured by wrapping a piece of string around the rim of the pan. Once again, lightly oil the paper, push against the tin and oil once more as this will hold the paper to the sides of the pan.

## Separating Eggs

When separating eggs (that is, separating the white from the yolk), crack an egg in half lightly and cleanly over a bowl, being careful not to break the yolk and keeping it in the shell. Then tip the yolk backward and forward between the two shell halves, letting as much of the white as possible spill into the bowl. Keep or discard the yolk and/or the white as needed. Make sure that you do not get any yolk in your whites because this will prevent successful whisking of the whites. It takes practice!

# Different Mixing Techniques

## Creaming

The creaming method—which means that the butter and sugar are first beaten or 'creamed' together—makes light cakes. A little care is needed for this method. Use a large

mixing bowl to beat the fat and sugar together until pale and fluffy. The eggs are gradually beaten in to form a slackened batter and the flour is folded in last, to stiffen up the mixture.

## Rubbing In

In this method, the fat is lightly worked into the flour between the fingers, as in pastry-making, until the mixture resembles fine crumbs. This can be done by hand or in a food processor. Enough liquid is stirred in to give a soft mixture that will drop easily from a spoon. This method is used for easy fruit cakes.

## All-In-One Mixtures

This 'one stage' method is quick and easy and is perfect for those new to baking, as it does not involve any complicated techniques. It is ideal for making light sponges, but soft tub-type margarine or softened butter at room temperature must be used. All the ingredients are simply placed in a large bowl and quickly beaten together for just a few minutes until smooth. Be careful not to overbeat, as this will make the mixture too wet. Self-rising flour with the addition of a little extra baking powder is vital for a good rise.

## The Melting Method

Cakes with a delicious moist, sticky texture, such as gingerbread, are made by this method. These cakes use a high proportion of sugar and syrup, which are gently warmed together in a pan with the fat, until the sugar has dissolved and the mixture is liquid. It is important to cool the hot melted mixture a little before beating in flour, eggs, and spices to make the batter, otherwise it will damage the power of the leavening agent.

# Icing Recipes

## Cream Cheese Frosting

**Covers the top of an 8-in round cake or 12 cupcakes**

4 tbsp. unsalted butter, softened
2⅓ cups confectioners' sugar, sifted
flavoring of choice
food colorings
½ cup cream cheese

Beat the butter and confectioners' sugar together until light and fluffy. Add the flavorings and colorings of choice and beat again. Add the cream cheese and beat until light and fluffy. Do not overbeat, however, or the mixture can become runny.

## Basic Buttercream

**Covers the top of an 8-in round cake or 12 cupcakes**

⅔ cup (1¼ sticks) unsalted butter, softened
1¾ cups confectioners' sugar, sifted
2 tbsp. hot milk or water
1 tsp. vanilla extract
food colorings of choice

Beat the butter until light and fluffy, then beat in the sifted confectioners' sugar and hot milk or water in two batches. Add the vanilla extract and any food colorings. Store chilled for up to 2 days in a lidded container.

## Chocolate Fudge Frosting

**Covers the top of an 8-in round cake or 12 cupcakes**

4 oz. semisweet chocolate, broken into pieces
4 tbsp. unsalted butter
1 large egg, beaten
1⅓ cups confectioners' sugar, sifted
½ tsp. vanilla extract

Place the chocolate and butter in a bowl over a pan of hot water and stir until melted. Remove from the heat and beat in the egg with the confectioners' sugar and vanilla. Beat until smooth and glossy, then use immediately, or let cool and thicken for a spreading consistency.

## Royal Icing

**Covers the top of an 8-in round cake or 12 cupcakes**

2 large egg whites
4 cups confectioners' sugar, sifted
2 tsp. lemon juice

Put the egg whites in a large bowl and beat lightly with a fork to break up the whites until foamy. Sift in half of the confectioners' sugar with the lemon juice and beat well with an electric mixer for 4 minutes, or by hand with a wooden spoon for about 10 minutes, until smooth.

Gradually sift in the remaining sugar and beat again until thick, smooth, and brilliant white and the icing forms soft peaks when flicked up with a spoon. Keep the royal icing covered with a clean, damp cloth until you are ready to use it, or store in the refrigerator in a sealed plastic container until needed. If making royal icing ahead of time to use later, beat it again before use to remove any air bubbles that may have formed in the mixture.

## Glacé Icing

**Covers the top of an 8-in round cake or 12 cupcakes**

1¾ cups confectioners' sugar
few drops lemon juice, or vanilla or almond extract
2–3 tbsp. boiling water
liquid food coloring

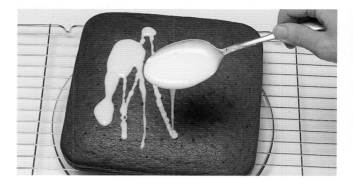

Sift the confectioners' sugar into a bowl and add the chosen flavoring. Gradually stir in enough water to mix to a consistency of thick cream. Beat with a wooden spoon until the icing is thick enough to coat the back of the spoon. Add coloring, if liked, and use at once because the icing will begin to form a skin.

## Apricot Glaze

**Covers two 8-in round cakes (tops) or 24 cupcakes**

scant 1½ cups apricot jelly
3 tbsp. water
1 tsp. lemon juice

Place the jelly, water, and juice in a heavy saucepan and heat gently, stirring, until soft and melted. Boil rapidly for 1 minute, then press through a fine strainer with the back of a

wooden spoon. Discard the pieces of fruit. Use immediately for glazing or sticking on almond paste, or pour into a clean jar or plastic container, seal, and store in the refrigerator for up to 3 months.

## Almond Paste

**Covers two 8-in round cakes (tops) or 24 cupcakes**

1 cup confectioners' sugar, sifted
⅔ cup superfine sugar
2⅓ cups ground almonds
1 large egg
1 tsp. lemon juice

Stir the sugars and ground almonds together in a bowl. Whisk the egg and lemon juice together and mix into the dry ingredients.

Knead until the paste is smooth. Wrap tightly in plastic wrap or foil to keep airtight and store in the refrigerator until needed. The paste can be made 2–3 days ahead of time, but, after that, it will start to dry out and become difficult to handle.

To use the almond paste, knead on a surface lightly dusted with confectioners' sugar until soft and pliable. Brush the top of each cake with apricot glaze. Roll out the paste and cut out disks large enough to cover the tops of the cakes. Press onto the cakes.

## Rolling Fondant

**Covers the top of an 8-in round cake or 12 cupcakes, or use for decorations**

1 large egg white
1 tbsp. liquid glucose
2¾ cups confectioners' sugar, sifted

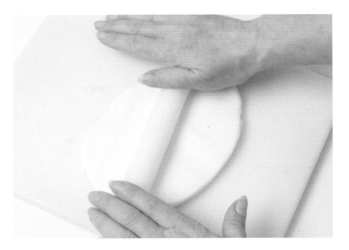

Place the egg white and liquid glucose in a large mixing bowl and stir together with a fork, breaking up the egg white. Add the confectioners' sugar gradually, mixing in with a palette knife until the mixture binds together and forms a ball. Turn the ball of fondant out onto a clean surface dusted with confectioners' sugar and knead for 5 minutes until soft but firm enough to roll out. If the fondant is too soft, knead in a little more confectioners' sugar until the mixture is pliable.

To color, knead in paste food coloring. Do not use liquid food coloring because this is not suitable and will make the fondant turn limp.

To use, roll out thinly on a clean surface dusted with confectioners' sugar and cut out a disk large enough to cover the top of each cake. Brush the almond paste (if using as a layer under the fondant) with a little cold boiled water or a clear liqueur, such as kirsch, then press onto the cake and press the fondant disk on top of the almond paste. Or coat the cakes with a little buttercream and press down the fondant disk on top.

To mold, knead lightly and roll out thinly on a surface dusted with confectioners' sugar. Cut out flat shapes, then mold into three-dimensional shapes with your fingertips; let dry for 24 hours in egg cartons lined with plastic wrap.

# Special Occasion
## & Dessert
## Cakes

# Sauternes & Olive Oil Cake

## Cuts into 8–10 slices

**1 cup all-purpose flour, plus extra for dusting**
**4 large eggs**
**½ cup superfine sugar**
**2 tsp. grated lemon zest**
**2 tsp. grated orange zest**
**2 tbsp. Sauternes or other sweet dessert wine**
**3 tbsp. good-quality extra-virgin olive oil**
**4 ripe peaches**
**1–2 tsp. soft brown sugar, or to taste**
**1 tbsp. lemon juice**
**confectioners' sugar, to dust**

1. Preheat the oven to 275°F. Grease and line a 10-inch springform pan. Sift the flour onto a large sheet of wax paper and set aside. Using a freestanding electric mixer, beat the eggs and sugar together until pale and stiff. Add the lemon and orange zest.

2. Turn the speed to low, and pour the flour from the paper in a slow, steady stream onto the egg and sugar mixture. Add the wine and olive oil, and switch the machine off, as the olive oil should not be incorporated completely.

3. Fold the mixture very gently three or four times so that the ingredients are just incorporated. Pour the mixture into the pan, and cook in the oven for 20–25 minutes, without opening the door for at least 15 minutes. Test if cooked by pressing the top lightly with a finger—if it springs back, remove from the oven. If not, cook for longer.

4. Let the cake cool in the pan on a wire rack. Remove the cake from the pan when cool enough to handle. Peel the peaches and cut into segments. Toss with the brown sugar and lemon juice, and set aside. When the cake is cold, dust with confectioners' sugar, cut into wedges, and serve with the peaches.

# Peach & White Chocolate Gateau

## Cuts into 8–10 slices

¾ cup (1½ sticks) unsalted
  butter, softened
2 tsp. grated orange zest
¾ cup superfine sugar
3 large eggs
3½ oz white chocolate,
  melted and cooled
2 cups self-rising flour, sifted
1 cup heavy cream
⅓ cup confectioners' sugar

For the filling and topping:
2 peeled and chopped ripe
  peaches
2 tbsp. peach or orange
  liqueur
1 cup heavy cream
⅓ cup confectioners' sugar
1 cup toasted and chopped
  hazelnuts

1. Preheat the oven to 325°F. Lightly grease and line a deep
   9-inch round cake pan. Cream the butter, orange zest, and
   sugar together until light and fluffy. Add the eggs, one at a
   time, beating well after each addition, then beat in the cooled
   white chocolate.

2. Add the flour and ¾ cup of water in two batches. Spoon into
   the pan and bake in the oven for 1½ hours or until firm. Let
   stand for at least 5 minutes before turning out onto a wire
   rack to cool completely.

3. For the filling, place the peaches in a bowl and pour over
   the liqueur. Let stand for 30 minutes. Whip the cream with
   the confectioners' sugar until soft peaks form, then fold in
   peach mixture.

4. Split the cake into three layers, place one layer on a plate, and
   spread with half the peach. Top with a second cake layer and
   spread with the remaining filling. Top with remaining cake.
   Whip the cream and confectioners' sugar together until soft
   peaks form. Spread over the top and sides of the cake. Press
   hazelnuts into the side of the cake and, if desired, sprinkle a
   few on top. Serve cut into slices. Store in refrigerator.

# Supreme Chocolate Gateau

Cuts into 10–12 slices

1½ cups self-rising flour, sifted
1½ tsp. baking powder, sifted
3 tbsp. unsweetened cocoa, sifted
¾ cup (1½ sticks) butter, softened
¾ cup superfine sugar
3 extra-large eggs

To decorate:
12 oz. semisweet dark chocolate
1 gelatin leaf
1 cup heavy cream
6 tbsp. butter
unsweetened cocoa, for dusting

1. Preheat the oven to 350°F. Lightly grease and line three 8-inch round cake pans.

2. Place all the cake ingredients into a bowl and beat together until thick. Add a little warm water if too thick. Divide the batter evenly among the prepared pans. Bake in the preheated oven for 35–40 minutes until a toothpick inserted in the center comes out clean. Cool on wire racks.

3. Very gently, heat 2 tablespoons of hot water with 2 oz. of the chocolate, and stir until combined. Remove from the heat and leave for 5 minutes.

4. Place the gelatin into a shallow dish and add 2 tablespoons cold water. Leave for 5 minutes, then squeeze out any excess water and add to the chocolate and water mixture. Stir until dissolved.

5. Whip the heavy cream until just thickened. Add the chocolate mixture and continue beating until soft peaks form. Leave until starting to set.

6. Place one of the cakes onto a serving plate and spread with half the cream mixture. Top with a second cake and the remaining cream, cover with the third cake, and chill in the refrigerator until set.

7. Melt half the remaining chocolate with the butter, and stir until smooth. Let thicken.

8. Melt the remaining chocolate. Cut 12 4-inch squares of foil. Spread the chocolate evenly over the squares to within 1 inch of the edges. Refrigerate for 3–4 minutes until just set but not brittle. Gather up the corners and crimp together. Return to the refrigerator until firm.

9. Spread the chocolate and butter mixture over the top and sides of the cake. Remove the foil from the giant curls and use to decorate the top of the cake. Dust with unsweetened cocoa and serve cut into wedges.

# White Chocolate & Raspberry Mousse Gateau

## Cuts into 8 slices

4 large eggs
½ cup superfine sugar
¾ cup all-purpose flour, sifted
¼ cup cornstarch, sifted
3 gelatin leaves
4 cups raspberries, thawed if frozen
14 oz. white chocolate

¾ cup fromage frais or reduced-fat sour cream
2 large egg whites
2 tbsp. superfine sugar
4 tbsp. raspberry or orange liqueur
¾ cup heavy cream
fresh raspberries, halved, to decorate

1. Preheat the oven to 375°F. Grease and line two 9-inch cake pans. Beat the eggs and sugar until thick and creamy and the whisk leaves a trail in the mixture. Fold in the flour and cornstarch, then divide among the pans. Bake in the preheated oven for 12–15 minutes or until risen and firm. Cool in the pans, then turn out onto wire racks.

2. Place the gelatin with 4 tablespoons of cold water in a dish and let soften for 5 minutes. Purée half the raspberries, press through a strainer, then heat until nearly boiling. Squeeze out excess water from the gelatin, add to the purée, and stir until dissolved. Set aside.

3. Melt 6 oz. of the chocolate in a bowl set over a saucepan of simmering water. Let cool, then stir in the yogurt and purée. Beat the egg whites until stiff and beat in the sugar. Fold into the raspberry mixture with the rest of the raspberries.

4. Line the sides of a 9-inch springform pan with nonstick parchment paper. Place one layer of sponge in the bottom and sprinkle with half the liqueur. Pour in the raspberry mixture and top with the second sponge. Brush with the remaining liqueur. Press down and chill in the refrigerator for 4 hours. Unmold onto a plate.

5. Cut a strip of double-thick nonstick parchment paper to fit around the cake and stand ½ inch higher. Melt the remaining white chocolate and spread thickly onto the paper. Leave until just setting. Wrap around the cake and freeze for 15 minutes. Peel away the paper. Whip the cream until thick and spread over the top. Decorate with raspberries.

# Pink Candle Cupcakes

**Makes 12**

⅔ cup fresh raspberries
⅔ cup (1¼ stick) butter, softened
⅔ cup superfine sugar
1½ cups self-rising flour
3 large eggs
1 tsp. vanilla extract

**To decorate:**
**1 batch cream cheese frosting (*see* page 23)**
**pink liquid food coloring**
**small pink candles**

1. Preheat the oven to 350°F. Line a muffin pan with 12
   paper baking cups.

2. Press the raspberries through a strainer to make a purée.
   Cream the butter and sugar in a bowl, then sift in the
   flour. In another bowl, beat the eggs with the vanilla
   extract, then add to the butter and sugar mixture. Beat
   until smooth, then fold in the purée. Spoon into the
   baking cups, filling them three-quarters full.

3. Bake for about 18 minutes until firm to the touch
   in the center. Turn out to cool on a wire rack.

4. Color the frosting pink with a few dots of food
   coloring. Place in a decorating bag fitted with a star
   tip and pipe large swirls on top of each cupcake.
   Top each cupcake with a tiny candle. Keep for 3 days
   in an airtight container in a cool place.

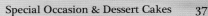

# Celebration Fruit Cake

Cuts into 16 slices

½ cup (1 stick) butter or margarine
1½ cups dark brown sugar
13 oz. canned crushed pineapple
1 cup raisins
1 cup golden raisins
½ cup finely chopped crystallized ginger
½ cup coarsely chopped candied cherries
½ cup diced candied peel
2 cups self-rising flour
1 tsp. baking soda
2 tsp. pumpkin pie spice
1 tsp. ground cinnamon
½ tsp. salt
2 extra-large eggs, beaten

For the topping:
⅔ cup lightly toasted pecan or walnut halves
½ cup red, green, and yellow candied cherries
¾ cup small pitted prunes or dates
2 tbsp. honey

1. Preheat the oven to 325°F. Heat the butter and sugar in a saucepan until the sugar has dissolved, stirring often.

2. Add the pineapple and juice, dried fruits, and peel. Bring to a boil, simmer for 3 minutes, stirring occasionally, then remove from the heat to cool completely.

3. Lightly grease and line the bottom of an 8-inch, round springform pan with nonstick parchment paper. Sift the flour, baking soda, spices, and salt into a bowl.

4. Add the boiled fruit mixture to the flour with the eggs and mix. Spoon into the pan and smooth the top. Bake in the preheated oven for 1¼ hours or until a skewer inserted into the center comes out clean. If the cake is browning too quickly, cover loosely with foil and reduce the oven temperature. Remove and cool completely before removing from the pan and discarding the lining paper.

5. Arrange the nuts, cherries, and prunes or dates in an attractive pattern on top of the cake. Heat the honey, and brush over the topping to glaze. Alternatively, toss the nuts and fruits in the warm honey and spread evenly over the top of the cake. Cool completely, and store in a sealed container for a day or two to allow the flavor to develop.

# Marzipan Cake

Cuts into 12–14 slices

4 cups blanched almonds
2¼ cups confectioners' sugar
  (includes sugar for dusting and rolling)
4 large egg whites
1 small plain sponge cake
2 tbsp. Marsala or other Italian dessert wine
1 cup ricotta cheese
¼ cup superfine sugar
2 tsp. grated lemon zest
⅓ cup chopped dried candied peel
1 tbsp. finely chopped glacé cherries
15 oz. canned peach halves, drained
1 cup heavy cream

1. Grind the almonds in a food processor until fairly fine. Mix with 1¾ cups of the confectioners' sugar. Beat the egg whites until stiff, then fold into the almond mixture to form a stiff dough. It will be quite sticky but will firm up as it rests. Leave for 30 minutes.

2. Dust a work surface with some of the remaining confectioners' sugar. Roll out two-thirds of the marzipan into a large sheet to a thickness of ¼ inch. Use to line a sloping-sided baking dish with a bottom measuring 8 x 10 inches. Trim the edges and put any trimmings with the rest of the marzipan.

3. Cut the cake into thin slices, and make a layer of sponge to cover the bottom of the marzipan. Sprinkle with the wine. Beat the ricotta with the sugar, and add the lemon zest, candied peel, and cherries. Spread this over the sponge. Slice the peaches and put them on top of the ricotta. Whip the cream and spread it over the peaches. Roll out the remaining marzipan, and lay it over the cream to seal the whole cake, pressing down gently to remove any air. Press the edges of the marzipan together. Chill in the refrigerator for 2 hours. Turn the cake out onto a serving plate, and dust generously with confectioners' sugar. Slice thickly and serve.

# Christmas Cranberry Chocolate Roulade

## Cuts into 12–14 slices

**5 extra-large eggs, separated**
**3 tbsp. unsweetened cocoa, sifted, plus extra for dusting**
**1 cup confectioners' sugar, sifted, plus extra for dusting**
**¼ tsp. cream of tartar**

**For the frosting:**
**1¼ cups heavy cream**
**12 oz. semisweet dark chocolate, chopped**
**2 tbsp. brandy (optional)**

**For the filling:**
**¾ cup cranberry sauce**
**1–2 tbsp. brandy (optional)**
**⅔ cup heavy cream, whipped to soft peaks**

**To decorate:**
**candied orange strips**
**dried cranberries**

1. Make the frosting first. Bring the cream to a boil over medium heat. Remove from the heat and add all of the chocolate, stirring until melted. Stir in the brandy, if desired, and strain into a medium bowl. Cool, then refrigerate for 6–8 hours.

2. Preheat the oven to 400°F. Lightly grease and line a 10 x 15-inch jelly-roll pan with nonstick parchment paper. Using an electric mixer, beat the egg yolks until thick and creamy. Slowly beat in the cocoa and half the confectioners' sugar, and set aside.

3. Beat the egg whites and tartar into soft peaks. Gradually beat in the remaining sugar until the mixture is stiff and glossy. Gently fold the yolk mixture into the egg whites with a metal spoon or rubber spatula. Spread evenly into the pan. Bake in the preheated oven for 15 minutes.

4. Remove, then invert onto a large sheet of wax paper dusted with cocoa. Cut off the crisp edges of the cake, then roll up. Leave on a wire rack until cool.

5. For the filling, heat the cranberry sauce with the brandy, if desired, until warm and spreadable. Unroll the cooled cake and spread with the cranberry sauce. Let cool and set. Carefully spoon the whipped cream over the surface and spread to within 1 inch of the edges. Roll the cake again. Transfer to a cake plate or tray.

6. Allow the chocolate ganache to soften at room temperature, then beat until soft and of a spreadable consistency. Spread over the roulade, and using a fork, mark the roulade with ridges to resemble tree bark. Dust with confectioners' sugar. Decorate with the candied orange strips and dried cranberries, and serve.

# Wild Strawberry & Rose Petal Jam Cake

Cuts into 8 slices

2½ cups all-purpose flour
1 tsp. baking powder
¼ tsp. salt
½ cup plus 2 tbsp.
  unsalted butter,
  softened
1 cup superfine sugar
2 large eggs, beaten
2 tbsp. rosewater
½ cup milk
frosted rose petals, to decorate

For the rose cream filling:
¾ cup heavy cream
1 tbsp. plain yogurt
2 tbsp. rosewater
1–2 tbsp. confectioners' sugar
½ cup rose petal or strawberry
  jelly, slightly warmed
¾ cup hulled wild strawberries
  or chopped baby strawberries

1. Preheat the oven to 350°F. Lightly grease and flour an
   8-inch, round, nonstick cake pan. Sift the flour, baking
   powder, and salt into a bowl, and set aside.

2. Beat the butter and sugar until light and fluffy. Beat in the
   eggs, a little at a time, then stir in the rosewater. Gently fold
   in the flour mixture and milk, and mix lightly together.
   Spoon into the pan, spreading evenly and smoothing the top.

3. Bake in the oven for 25–30 minutes or until well risen and
   golden, and the center springs back when pressed with a
   clean finger. Remove and cool, then remove from the pan.

4. For the filling, beat the cream, yogurt, half the rosewater, and
   1 tablespoon of confectioners' sugar until soft peaks form.
   Split the cake horizontally in half, and sprinkle with the
   remaining rosewater. Spread the warmed jelly on the base.
   Top with half the whipped cream mixture, then sprinkle
   with half the strawberries. Place the remaining cake on top.
   Spread with the remaining cream. Decorate with the rose
   petals. Dust the cake with a little confectioners' sugar. Serve.

# Black Forest Gateau

## Cuts into 10–12 slices

1 cup plus 2 tbsp. (2¼ sticks) butter
1 tbsp. instant coffee grounds
1½ cups hot water
7 oz. semisweet dark chocolate, chopped or broken
1¼ cups superfine sugar
2 cups self-rising flour
1¼ cups all-purpose flour

½ cup unsweetened cocoa
2 large eggs
2 tsp. vanilla extract
2 14-oz. cans pitted cherries in juice
2 tsp. arrowroot
2 cups heavy cream
¼ cup kirsch

1. Preheat the oven to 300°F. Lightly grease and line a deep 9-inch cake pan.

2. Melt the butter in a large saucepan. Blend the coffee with the hot water, add to the butter with the chocolate and sugar, and heat gently, stirring until smooth. Pour into a large bowl and leave until just warm.

3. Sift together the flours and unsweetened cocoa. Using an electric mixer, beat the warm chocolate mixture on a low speed, then gradually beat in the dry ingredients. Beat in the eggs one at a time, then add the vanilla extract.

4. Pour the batter into the prepared pan and bake in the preheated oven for 1 hour and 45 minutes or until firm and a toothpick inserted into the center comes out clean. Leave the cake in the pan for 5 minutes to cool slightly before turning out onto a wire rack.

5. Place the cherries and their juice in a small saucepan and heat gently. Blend the arrowroot with 2 teaspoons of water until smooth, then stir into the cherries. Cook, stirring until the liquid thickens. Simmer very gently for 2 minutes, then leave until cooled.

6. Beat the heavy cream until thick. Trim the top of the cake if necessary, then split the cake into three layers. Brush the bottom of the cake with half the kirsch. Top with a layer of cream and one-third of the cherries. Repeat the layering, then place the third layer on top.

7. Set aside a little cream for decorating and use the remainder to cover the top and sides of the cake. Pipe a decorative edge around the cake, then arrange the remaining cherries in the center and serve.

# Chocolate Holly Leaf Cupcakes

## Makes 12

½ cup superfine sugar
½ cup (8 tbsp.) soft
  tub margarine
2 large eggs
1 cup self-rising flour
½ tsp. baking powder
¼ cup semisweet dark or
  milk chocolate chips

**To decorate:**
12 holly leaves, washed and dried
4 tbsp. unsalted butter, softened
3 cups confectioners' sugar, sifted
3 oz. semisweet dark chocolate, melted
½ cup full-fat cream cheese
2 oz. milk chocolate, melted
  and cooled
1 tsp. vanilla extract

1. Preheat the oven to 375°F. Line a muffin pan with 12 paper baking cups.

2. Place all the cupcake ingredients except the chocolate chips in a large bowl and beat with an electric mixer for about 2 minutes until smooth. Fold in the chocolate chips, then fill the baking cups halfway up with the mixture. Bake for about 15 minutes until firm, risen, and golden. Remove to a wire rack to cool.

3. To decorate the cupcakes, paint the underside of each holly leaf with the melted dark chocolate. Leave to dry out on nonstick parchment paper for 1 hour, or in the refrigerator for 30 minutes.

4. Beat the butter until soft, then gradually beat in the confectioners' sugar until light. Add the cream cheese and whisk until fluffy. Divide the mixture in half and beat the cooled melted milk chocolate into one half and the vanilla extract into the other half. Fit a decorating bag with a wide star tip and spoon chocolate icing on one side of the bag and the vanilla icing on the other. Pipe swirls on top of the cupcakes.

5. Peel the holly leaves away from the set chocolate and decorate the top of each cupcake with a chocolate leaf. Keep for 3 days in an airtight container in a cool place.

# Coffee & Walnut Gateau with Brandied Prunes

## Cuts into 10–12 slices

4 cups walnut pieces
½ cup self-rising flour
½ tsp. baking powder
1 tsp. instant coffee powder (not granules)
5 extra-large eggs, separated
¼ tsp. cream of tartar
½ cup plus 2 tbsp. superfine sugar
2 tbsp. sunflower oil
8 walnut halves, to decorate

For the prunes:
1½ cups pitted dried prunes
⅔ cup cold tea
3 tbsp. brandy

For the filling:
2½ cups heavy cream
4 tbsp. confectioners' sugar, sifted
2 tbsp. coffee-flavored liqueur

1. Preheat the oven to 350°F. Put the prunes in a small bowl with the tea and brandy, and let stand for 3–4 hours or overnight. Grease and line the bottoms of two 9-inch round cake pans.

2. Chop the walnut pieces in a food processor. Set aside a quarter of the nuts. Add the flour, baking powder, and coffee, and blend until finely ground.

3. Beat the egg whites with the cream of tartar until soft peaks form. Sprinkle in one third of the sugar, 2 tablespoons at a time, until stiff peaks form.

4. In another bowl, beat the egg yolks, oil, and the remaining sugar until thick. Using a metal spoon, alternately fold in the nut mixture and egg whites until just blended.

5. Divide the mixture evenly between the pans, smoothing the tops. Bake in the preheated oven for 30–35 minutes or until the top of the cakes spring back when lightly pressed with a clean finger. Remove from the oven and cool. Remove from the pans and discard the lining paper.

6. Drain the prunes, setting aside the soaking liquid. Dry on paper towels, then chop and set aside.

7. Beat the cream with the confectioners' sugar and liqueur until soft peaks form. Spoon an eighth of the cream into a pastry bag fitted with a star tip.

8. Cut the cake layers in half horizontally. Sprinkle each cut side with 1 tablespoon of the prune-soaking liquid. Sandwich the cakes together with half of the cream and all of the prunes.

9. Spread the remaining cream around the sides of the cake and press in the chopped walnuts. Pipe rosettes around the edge of the cake. Decorate with walnut halves and serve.

# Orange Fruit Cake

## Cuts into 10–12 slices

2 cups self-rising flour
2 tsp. baking powder
1 cup superfine sugar
1 cup (2 sticks) butter, softened
4 extra-large eggs
grated zest of 1 orange
2 tbsp. orange juice
2–3 tbsp. Cointreau
1 cup chopped nuts
Cape gooseberries, blueberries,
  raspberries, and mint sprigs,
  to decorate
confectioners' sugar, to dust (optional)

For the filling:
2 cups heavy cream
⅓ cup Greek yogurt
½ tsp. vanilla extract
2–3 tbsp. Cointreau
1 tbsp. confectioners' sugar
3½ cups orange fruits, such
  as mango, peach,
  nectarine, papaya, and
  yellow plums

1. Preheat the oven to 350°F. Lightly grease and line the bottom
   of a 10-inch deep cake pan with nonstick parchment paper.

2. Sift the flour and baking powder into a bowl, then stir in the
   sugar. Make a well in the center and add the butter, eggs,
   grated zest, and orange juice. Beat until blended and a smooth
   batter is formed. Turn into the pan and smooth the top. Bake
   in the oven for 35–45 minutes or until golden and the sides
   begin to shrink from the edge of the pan. Remove, cool
   before removing from the pan, and discard the lining paper.
   Using a serrated knife, slice off the top third of the cake,
   cutting horizontally. Sprinkle the cut sides with the Cointreau.

3. For the filling, whip the cream and yogurt with the vanilla
   extract, Cointreau, and confectioners' sugar until soft peaks
   form. Chop the orange fruits and fold into the cream. Spoon
   some mixture onto the bottom cake layer. Transfer to a plate.

4. Cover with the top layer of sponge cake and spread the
   remaining cream mixture over the top of the cake. Press the
   nuts into the sides and decorate the top with the Cape
   gooseberries, blueberries, and raspberries. If desired, dust top
   with confectioners' sugar, and serve.

# Almond Angel Cake with Amaretto Cream

Cuts into 10–12 slices

1½ cups confectioners' sugar,
  plus 2–3 tbsp.
1½ cups all-purpose flour
1½ cups egg whites (about 10
  extra-large egg whites)
1½ tsp. cream of tartar
½ tsp. vanilla extract

1 tsp. almond extract
¼ tsp. salt
1 scant cup superfine sugar
¾ cup heavy cream
2 tablespoons Amaretto liqueur
fresh raspberries, to decorate

1. Preheat the oven to 350°F. Sift together the 1½ cups confectioners' sugar and flour. Stir to blend, then sift again.

2. Using an electric mixer, beat the egg whites, cream of tartar, vanilla extract, ½ teaspoon of almond extract, and salt on medium speed until soft peaks form. Gradually add the superfine sugar, 2 tablespoons at a time, beating well after each addition until stiff peaks form.

3. Sift about one-third of the flour mixture over the egg-white mixture, and, using a metal spoon or rubber spatula, gently fold into the egg white mixture. Repeat, folding the flour mixture into the egg white mixture in two more batches. Spoon into an ungreased angel food cake pan or 10-inch tube pan.

4. Bake in the preheated oven until risen and golden on top and the surface springs back quickly when gently pressed. Immediately invert the cake pan and cool completely in the pan. When cool, run a sharp knife around the edge and the center ring to loosen the cake from the edge. Using the fingertips, ease the cake from the pan and invert onto a cake plate. Thickly dust the cake with the extra confectioners' sugar.

5. Whip the cream with the remaining almond extract, Amaretto liqueur, and a little more confectioners' sugar until soft peaks form.

6. Fill a piping bag fitted with a star tip with half the cream, and pipe around the bottom of the cake. Decorate the edge with the fresh raspberries, and serve the remaining cream separately.

# Black & White Torte

Cuts into 8–10 slices

**4 large eggs**
**⅔ cup sugar**
**½ cup cornstarch**
**½ cup all-purpose flour**
**½ cup self-rising flour**
**3 cups heavy cream**
**5 oz. semisweet dark chocolate, chopped**
**11 oz. white chocolate, chopped**
**6 tbsp. Grand Marnier or other orange-flavored liqueur**
**unsweetened cocoa, for dusting**

1. Preheat the oven to 350°F. Lightly grease and line a 9-inch round cake pan. Beat the eggs and sugar in a large bowl until thick and creamy. Sift together the cornstarch, all-purpose flour, and self-rising flour three times, then lightly fold into the egg mixture. Spoon the batter into the pan and bake in the oven for 35–40 minutes or until firm. Turn out onto a wire rack and let cool.

2. Place 1 cup of the heavy cream in a saucepan and bring to a boil. Immediately remove from the heat, and add the semisweet dark chocolate and an additional tablespoon of the liqueur. Stir until smooth. Repeat, using the remaining cream, white chocolate, and liqueur. Chill in the refrigerator for 2 hours, then beat each mixture until thick and creamy. Place the dark chocolate mixture in a decorating bag fitted with a plain tip, and place half the white chocolate mixture in a separate decorating bag fitted with a plain tip. Set aside the remaining white chocolate mixture.

3. Split the cake horizontally into two layers. Brush or drizzle the remaining liqueur over the cakes. Put one layer onto a plate. Pipe alternating rings of white and dark chocolate mixture to cover the first layer of cake. Use the white chocolate mixture to cover the top and sides of the cake. Dust with unsweetened cocoa, cut into slices, and serve. Store in the refrigerator.

# Sachertorte

## Cuts into 10–12 slices

5 oz. semisweet dark chocolate
⅔ cup (1¼ sticks) unsalted
  butter, softened
½ cup superfine sugar,
  plus 2 tbsp.
3 large eggs, separated
1¼ cups all-purpose flour, sifted

**To decorate:**
⅔ cup apricot jelly
4 oz. semisweet dark
  chocolate, chopped
1 stick unsalted butter
1 oz. milk chocolate

1. Preheat the oven to 350°F. Lightly grease and line a deep 9-inch cake pan. Melt the chocolate in a heatproof bowl set over a saucepan of simmering water. Stir in 1 tablespoon of water and let cool. Beat the butter and ½ cup of the sugar together until light and fluffy. Beat in the egg yolks, one at a time, beating well between each addition. Stir in the melted chocolate, then the flour.

2. In a clean, grease-free bowl, beat the egg whites until stiff peaks form, then beat in the remaining sugar. Fold into the chocolate mixture and spoon into the pan. Bake in the oven for 30 minutes or until firm. Leave for 5 minutes, then turn out onto a wire rack to cool. Leave upside down.

3. To decorate, split the cake in two and place one half on a plate. Heat the jelly and rub through a fine strainer. Brush half the jelly onto the first cake half, then cover with the remaining cake layer and brush with the remaining jelly. Leave for 1 hour or until the jelly has set. Place the semisweet dark chocolate and the butter into a heatproof bowl set over a saucepan of simmering water, and heat until the chocolate has melted. Stir occasionally until smooth, then leave until thickened. Use to cover the cake.

4. Melt the milk chocolate in a heatproof bowl set over a saucepan of simmering water. Place in a small waxed decorating bag and snip a small hole at the tip. Pipe "Sacher" with a large "S" on the top. Let set at room temperature.

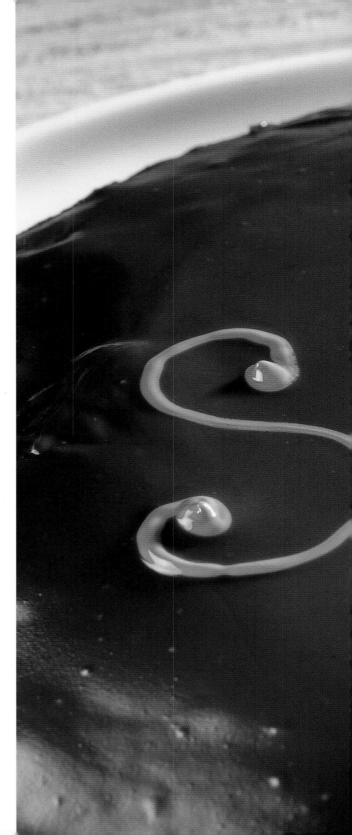

# Christmas Cake

## Cuts into 12–14 slices

5 cups mixed dried fruit
⅓ cup rinsed and halved candied cherries
3 tbsp. brandy or orange juice
finely grated zest and juice of 1 lemon
1 cup (2 sticks) room temperature butter
1 cup packed brown sugar
4 large eggs, beaten
1¾ cups all-purpose flour
1 tbsp. molasses
1 tbsp. pumpkin pie spice

**To decorate:**
2–4 tbsp. brandy (optional)
4 tbsp. apricot jelly
1½ lb almond paste
2 lb 3 oz ready-to-use
  rolled fondant
confectioners' sugar,
  for dusting
decorations and ribbon

1. Place the mixed dried fruit and cherries in a bowl and sprinkle over the brandy or orange juice and the lemon zest and juice. Stir and let soak for 2–4 hours.

2. Preheat the oven to 300°F. Grease and double-line the bottom and sides of an 8-inch round deep cake pan. Beat the butter and sugar together until soft and fluffy. Beat the eggs in gradually, adding 1 teaspoon flour with each addition. Stir in the molasses, then sift in the rest of the flour and the spice. Add the soaked fruit and stir until the mixture is smooth.

3. Spoon into the pan and smooth the top level. Bake for 1 hour, then reduce the temperature to 275°F and bake for an additional 2–2½ hours until a skewer inserted into the center comes out clean. Let the cake cool in the pan, then, when completely cold, remove from the pan, wrap in wax paper and then in foil, and store in a cool place for 1–3 months.

4. To decorate, brush the cake all over with brandy, if using. Heat the jelly and brush over the top and sides. Roll out one-third of the almond paste and cut into a disk the size of the top of the cake, using the empty pan as a guide. Place the disk on top. Roll the remaining paste into a strip long enough to cover the sides of the cake and press on. Let the almond paste dry out for 2 days in a cool place.

5. On a surface dusted with confectioners' sugar, roll out the fondant to a circle large enough to cover the top and sides of the cake. Brush 1 tablespoon brandy, or cold boiled water, over the almond paste and place the fondant on top. Smooth down and trim. Make a border from tiny balls of fondant and decorate.

# Apple & Cinnamon Crisp-Top Cake

Cuts into 8 slices

**For the topping:**
¼ lb. apples, peeled
1 tbsp. lemon juice
1 cup self-rising flour
1 tsp. ground cinnamon
6 tbsp. butter or margarine
6 tbsp. brown sugar
1 tbsp. milk

**For the base:**
½ cup (1 stick) butter or
 margarine
4 tbsp. superfine sugar
2 large eggs
1 cup plus 3 tbsp.
 self-rising flour
cream or freshly made
 custard sauce, to serve

1. Preheat the oven to 350 °F. Lightly grease and line the bottom of an 8-inch round cake pan with wax paper or parchment paper.

2. Finely chop the apples and mix with the lemon juice. Set aside while making the cake.

3. For the crisp topping, sift the flour and cinnamon together into a large bowl. Rub the butter or margarine into the flour and cinnamon until the mixture resembles coarse bread crumbs. Stir the brown sugar into the bread crumbs and set aside.

4. For the base, cream the butter or margarine and sugar together until light and fluffy. Gradually beat the eggs into the sugar-and-butter mixture, a little at a time, until all the egg has been added. Sift the flour, and gently fold in with a metal spoon or rubber spatula.

5. Spoon into the bottom of the prepared cake pan. Arrange the apple pieces on top, then lightly stir the milk into the crisp mixture. Sprinkle the crumble over the apples, and bake in the preheated oven for 1½ hours. Serve cold with cream or custard sauce.

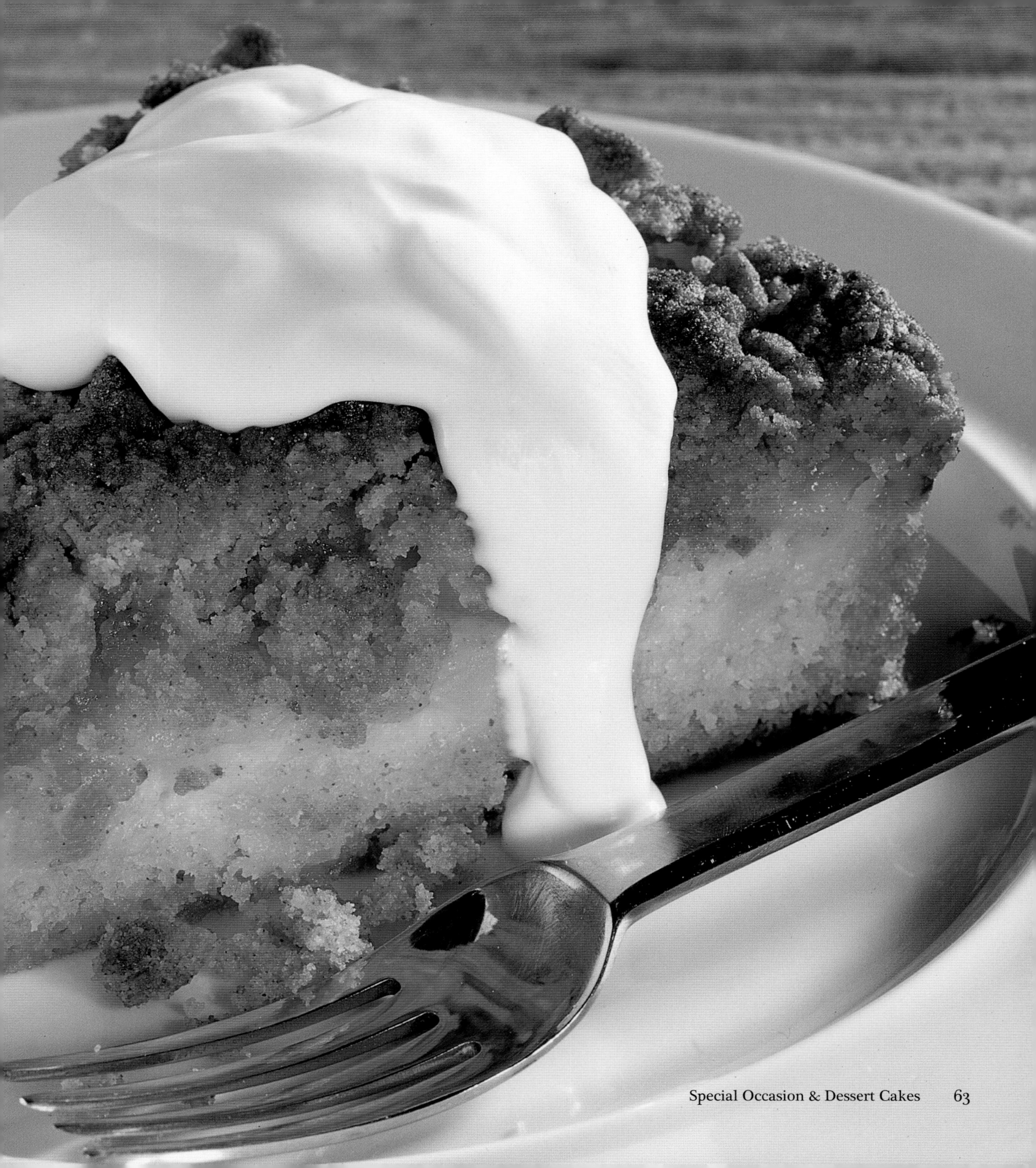

# Chocolate
## Cakes

# Double Chocolate Cake with Cinnamon

## Cuts into 10 slices

6 tbsp. unsweetened cocoa
1 tsp. ground cinnamon
2 cups self-rising flour
1 cup (2 sticks) unsalted
  butter or margarine
1 cup superfine sugar
4 extra-large eggs

For the filling and topping:
4 oz. white chocolate
¼ cup heavy cream
1 oz. semisweet
  dark chocolate

1. Preheat the oven to 375°F. Lightly grease and line the bottoms of two 8-inch layer cake pans with baking parchment. Sift the cocoa, cinnamon, and flour together, and set aside.

2. In a large bowl, cream the butter or margarine and sugar until light and fluffy. Beat in the eggs, a little at a time, until they are all incorporated and the mixture is smooth. If it looks curdled at any point, beat in a tablespoon of the sifted flour.

3. Using a rubber spatula or metal spoon, fold the sifted flour and cocoa into the egg mixture until mixed well.

4. Divide between the two cake pans, and level the surface. Bake in the preheated oven for 25–30 minutes until springy to the touch, and a toothpick inserted into the center of the cake comes out clean. Turn out onto a wire rack to cool.

5. To make the filling, coarsely break the white chocolate and heat the cream very gently in a small saucepan. Add the chocolate, stirring until melted. Let cool, then using half of the cooled white chocolate, sandwich the cakes together.

6. Top the cake with the rest of the white chocolate. Grate the semisweet dark chocolate over the top, and serve.

# Dark Chocolate Layered Torte

Cuts into 10–12 slices

¾ cup (1½ sticks) butter
1 tbsp. instant coffee granules
5 oz. semisweet dark chocolate
1½ cups superfine sugar
1¼ cups self-rising flour
1 cup all-purpose flour
2 tbsp. unsweetened cocoa
2 large eggs
1 tsp. vanilla extract

For the filling and covering:
7½ oz. semisweet dark chocolate, melted
½ cup (1 stick) butter, melted
⅓ cup confectioners' sugar, sifted
2 tsp. raspberry jelly
2½ tbsp. chocolate liqueur
¾ cup toasted slivered almonds

1. Preheat the oven to 300°F. Lightly grease and line a 9-inch square cake pan.

2. Melt the butter in a saucepan, remove from the heat, and stir in the coffee granules and 1 cup hot water. Add the semisweet dark chocolate and sugar, and stir until smooth, then pour into a bowl.

3. In another bowl, sift together the flours and unsweetened cocoa. Using an electric mixer, beat the sifted mixture into the chocolate mixture until smooth.

4. Beat in the eggs and vanilla extract. Pour into the pan and bake in the preheated oven for 1¼ hours or until firm. Leave for at least 5 minutes before turning out onto a wire rack to cool.

5. Meanwhile, mix together 7 oz. of the melted semisweet dark chocolate with the butter and confectioners' sugar, and beat until smooth. Let cool, then beat again. Set aside 4–5 tablespoons of the chocolate filling.

6. Cut the cooled cake in half horizontally, then split each half in three. Place one cake layer on a serving plate and spread thinly with the jelly, and then a thin layer of dark chocolate filling. Top with a second cake layer and sprinkle with a little liqueur, then spread thinly with filling. Repeat with remaining cake layers, liqueur, and filling.

7. Chill in the refrigerator for 2–3 hours or until firm. Cover the cake with the chocolate filling and press the slivered almonds into the sides of the cake.

8. Place the remaining melted chocolate in a nonstick parchment paper decorating bag. Snip a small hole in the tip and pipe thin lines, ¾ inch apart, crosswise over the cake. Drag a toothpick lengthwise through the frosting in alternating directions to create a feathered effect. Serve.

# Chocolate Orange Fudge Cake

## Cuts into 8–10 slices

⅔ cup unsweetened cocoa
1 tbsp. grated orange zest
3 cups self-rising flour
2 tsp. baking powder
1 tsp. baking soda
½ tsp. salt
1 cup firmly packed
  light brown sugar
3¼ cup (1½ sticks) butter,
  softened

3 large eggs
1 tsp. vanilla extract
1⅛ cup sour cream
6 tbsp. butter
6 tbsp. milk
zest of 1 orange, in thin strips
6 tbsp. unsweetened cocoa
2¼ cups confectioners'
  sugar, sifted

1. Preheat the oven to 350°F. Lightly grease and line two
   9-inch layer cake pans with nonstick parchment paper.
   Blend the unsweetened cocoa and ¼ cup of boiling water
   until smooth. Stir in the orange zest and set aside. Sift
   together the flour, baking powder, baking soda, and salt, then
   set aside. Cream together the sugar and softened butter, and
   beat in the eggs, one at a time, then the cocoa mixture and
   vanilla extract. Finally, stir in the flour mixture and the sour
   cream in alternating spoonfuls.

2. Divide the batter among the pans and bake in the oven for 35
   minutes or until the edges of the cake pull away from the pan
   and the tops spring back when lightly pressed. Cool in the
   pans for 10 minutes, then turn out onto wire racks until cold.

3. Gently heat the butter and milk with the pared orange zest.
   Simmer for 10 minutes, stirring occasionally. Remove from the
   heat and discard the orange zest. Pour the warm orange and
   milk mixture into a large bowl and stir in the unsweetened
   cocoa. Gradually beat in the sifted confectioners' sugar and
   beat until the frosting is smooth and spreadable. Place one cake
   onto a large serving plate. Top with about one-quarter of the
   frosting, place the second cake on top, then cover the cake
   with the remaining frosting. Serve.

# Easy Chocolate Cake

## Cuts into 8–10

3 oz. semisweet dark chocolate,
  broken into squares
1 scant cup milk
1 heaping cup packed
  dark brown sugar
6 tbsp. butter, softened
2 large eggs, beaten
1¼ cups all-purpose flour
½ tsp. vanilla extract
1 tsp. baking soda
¼ cup unsweetened cocoa

**For the topping and filling:**
½ cup (1 stick) unsalted butter
1¾ cups sifted confectioners' sugar
6 oz. (about 14) fresh
  strawberries, halved
tiny mint sprigs, to decorate

1. Preheat the oven to 350°F. Grease two 8-inch round cake pans and line the bottoms with nonstick parchment paper. Place the chocolate, milk, and ⅓ cup of the sugar in a heavy saucepan. Heat gently until the mixture has melted, then set aside to cool.

2. Place the butter and remaining sugar in a large bowl and beat with an electric mixer until light and fluffy. Gradually beat in the eggs, adding 1 teaspoon flour with each addition. Stir in the cooled melted chocolate mixture along with the vanilla extract. Sift in the flour, baking soda, and unsweetened cocoa, then fold into the mixture until smooth.

3. Spoon the batter into the pans and smooth level. Bake for about 30 minutes until it is firm to the touch and a toothpick inserted into the center comes out clean. Turn out to cool on a wire rack.

4. To decorate, beat the butter with the confectioners' sugar and 1 tablespoon warm water until light and fluffy, then place half in a pastry bag fitted with a star tip. Spread half the buttercream over one cake and scatter half the strawberries over it. Top with the other cake and spread the remaining buttercream over the top. Pipe a border of stars around the edge. Decorate with the remaining strawberries and the mint sprigs.

# Whole Orange & Chocolate Cake
# With Marmalade Cream

Cuts into 6–8 slices

**1 small scrubbed orange**
**2 large eggs, separated,**
  **plus 1 whole egg**
**1¼ cups superfine sugar**
**1 cup ground almonds**
**3 oz. semisweet dark chocolate, melted**

**To decorate:**
**½ cup heavy cream**
**¾ cup cream cheese**
**¼ cup confectioners' sugar**
**2 tbsp. orange marmalade**
**orange zest, to decorate**

1. Preheat the oven to 350°F. Lightly grease and line the bottom of a 9 x 5 x 3-inch loaf pan. Place the orange in a small saucepan, cover with cold water, and bring to a boil. Simmer for 1 hour or until completely soft. Drain and let cool.

2. Place 2 egg yolks, 1 whole egg, and the sugar in a heatproof bowl set over a saucepan of simmering water, and beat until doubled in bulk. Remove from the heat and continue to beat for 5 minutes until cooled.

3. Cut the whole orange in half and discard the seeds, then place in a food processor or blender and blend to a purée.

4. Carefully fold the purée into the egg yolk mixture with the ground almonds and melted chocolate.

5. Beat the egg whites until stiff peaks form. Fold a large spoonful of the egg whites into the chocolate mixture, then gently fold the remaining egg whites into the mixture. Pour into the prepared pan and bake in the preheated oven for 50 minutes or until firm and a toothpick inserted into the center comes out clean. Cool in the pan before turning out and carefully discarding the lining paper.

6. Meanwhile, whip the heavy cream until just thickened. In another bowl, blend the cream cheese with the confectioners' sugar and marmalade until smooth, then fold in the heavy cream. Chill the marmalade cream in the refrigerator until needed. Decorate with orange zest, cut in slices, and serve with the marmalade cream.

# Apricot & Almond Layer Cake

## Cuts into 8–10 slices

⅔ cup (1¼ sticks) unsalted
  butter, softened
½ cup sugar
5 large eggs, separated
5 oz. bittersweet chocolate,
  melted and cooled
1¼ cups self-rising flour, sifted
½ cup ground almonds
¾ cup confectioners' sugar, sifted
¾ cup apricot jelly
1 tbsp. amaretto liqueur

For the icing:
½ cup (1 stick) unsalted
  butter, melted
4 oz. semisweet dark
  chocolate, melted

1. Preheat the oven to 350°F. Lightly grease and line two
   9-inch round cake pans. Cream the butter and sugar
   together until light and fluffy, then beat in the egg yolks,
   one at a time, beating well after each addition. Stir in the
   cooled chocolate with 1 tablespoon of cooled boiled water,
   then fold in the flour and ground almonds.

2. Beat the egg whites until stiff, then gradually beat in the
   confectioners' sugar, beating well. Beat until stiff and glossy,
   then fold the egg whites into the chocolate mixture in two
   batches. Divide the batter among the pans and bake in the
   oven for 30–40 minutes or until firm. Leave for 5 minutes
   then turn out onto wire racks. Let cool completely.

3. Split the cakes in half. Gently heat the jelly, pass through a
   strainer, and stir in the amaretto liqueur. Place one cake
   layer onto a plate. Spread with a little of the jelly, then
   sandwich with the next layer. Repeat with all the layers and
   use any remaining jelly to brush over the entire cake. Leave
   until the jelly sets. Beat the butter and chocolate together
   until smooth, then cool at room temperature until thick
   enough to spread. Cover the top and sides of the cake with
   the chocolate icing, and let set before slicing and serving.

# Fruit & Spice Chocolate Slice

## Cuts into 10 slices

**3 cups self-rising flour**
**1 tsp. ground mixed spice**
**¾ cup (1½ sticks) butter, chilled**
**4 oz. semisweet dark chocolate, coarsely chopped**
**⅔ cup dried mixed fruit**
**¼ cup dried apricots, chopped**
**¾ cup chopped mixed nuts**
**1½ cups raw sugar**
**2 large eggs, lightly beaten**
**⅔ cup milk**

1. Preheat the oven to 350°F. Grease and line a deep 7-inch square pan with nonstick parchment paper. Sift the flour and mixed spice into a large bowl. Cut the butter into small squares and, using your hands, rub in until the mixture resembles fine bread crumbs.

2. Add the chocolate, dried mixed fruit, apricots, and nuts to the dry ingredients. Set aside 1 tablespoon of the sugar, then add the rest to the bowl and stir together. Add the eggs and half of the milk and mix together, then add enough of the remaining milk to give a soft dropping consistency.

3. Spoon the batter into the prepared pan, level the surface with the back of a spoon, and sprinkle with the raw sugar. Bake on the center shelf of the preheated oven for 50 minutes. Cover the top with foil to keep the cake from browning too much, and bake for an additional 30–40 minutes or until it is firm to the touch and a toothpick inserted into the center comes out clean.

4. Leave the cake in the pan for 10 minutes to cool slightly, then turn out onto a wire rack and let cool completely. Cut into 10 slices and serve. Store in an airtight container.

# Chocolate Mousse Cake

## Cuts into 8–10 slices

1 lb. semisweet dark chocolate, chopped
½ cup (1 stick) butter, softened
3 tbsp. brandy
9 extra-large eggs, separated
½ cup plus 2 tbsp. superfine sugar
1 tbsp. light cream and white chocolate curls, to decorate

For the chocolate glaze:
1 cup heavy cream
8 oz. semisweet dark chocolate, chopped
2 tbsp. brandy

1. Preheat the oven to 350°F. Lightly grease and line the bottoms of two 8-inch round springform pans with parchment paper. Melt the chocolate and butter in a bowl set over a saucepan of simmering water. Stir until smooth. Remove from the heat, and stir in the brandy.

2. Beat the egg yolks and the sugar, setting aside 2 tablespoons of the sugar, until thick and creamy. Slowly beat in the chocolate mixture until smooth and well blended. Beat the egg whites until soft peaks form, then sprinkle over the remaining sugar, and continue beating until stiff but not dry.

3. Fold a large spoonful of the egg whites into the chocolate mixture. Gently fold in the remaining egg whites. Divide about two-thirds of the mixture evenly between the pans, tapping to distribute the mixture evenly. Set aside the remaining third of the chocolate mousse mixture for the filling. Bake in the preheated oven for about 20 minutes or until well risen and set. Remove and cool for at least 1 hour.

4. Loosen the edges of the cake layers with a knife. Using your fingertips, lightly press the crusty edges down. Pour the rest of the mousse over one layer, spreading until even. Carefully unclip the side, remove the other cake from the pan, and gently invert onto the mousse, bottom-side up to make a flat top layer. Discard the lining paper and chill for 4–6 hours or until set.

5. To make the glaze, melt the cream and chocolate with the brandy in a heavy saucepan and stir until smooth. Cool until thickened. Unclip the side of the mousse cake pan and place on a wire rack. Pour over half the glaze and spread to cover. Let set, then decorate with chocolate curls. To serve, heat the remaining glaze, pour it around each slice, and dot with cream.

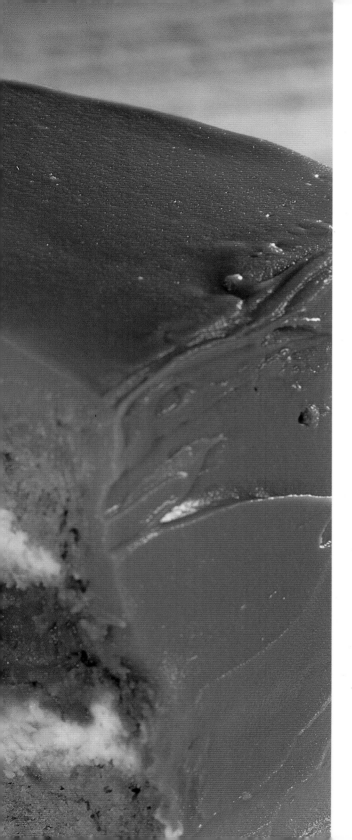

# Mocha Truffle Cake

## Cuts into 8–10 slices

**3 large eggs**
**½ cup superfine sugar**
**⅓ cup cornstarch**
**⅓ cup self-rising flour**
**2 tbsp. unsweetened cocoa**
**2 tbsp. milk**
**2 tbsp. coffee liqueur**
**3½ oz. white chocolate, melted and cooled**
**7 oz. semisweet dark chocolate, melted and cooled**
**2 cups heavy cream**
**7 oz. milk chocolate**
**7 tbsp. unsalted butter**

1. Preheat the oven to 350°F. Lightly grease and line a deep 9-inch round cake pan. Beat the eggs and sugar in a bowl until thick and creamy. Sift together the cornstarch, self-rising flour, and cocoa, and fold into the egg mixture. Spoon into the pan, and bake in the oven for 30 minutes or until firm. Turn out onto a wire rack and leave until cool. Split the cake horizontally into two layers. Mix together the milk and coffee liqueur, and brush onto the cake layers.

2. Stir the cooled white chocolate into one bowl and the cooled dark chocolate into another one. Whip the cream until soft peaks form, then divide among the two bowls and stir. Place one layer of cake in a 9-inch springform pan. Spread with half the white chocolate cream. Top with the dark chocolate cream, then the remaining white chocolate cream, and finally place the remaining cake layer on top. Chill in the refrigerator for 4 hours or until set.

3. Before serving, melt the milk chocolate and butter in a heatproof bowl set over a saucepan of simmering water. Stir until smooth. Remove from the heat and leave until thick enough to spread. Cover the top and sides of the cake. Let set, then chill in the refrigerator. Cut into slices and serve.

# Rich Devil's Food Cake

Cuts into 12–16 slices

4 cups all-purpose flour
1 tbsp. baking soda
½ tsp. salt
9 tbsp. unsweetened cocoa
1¼ cups milk
½ cup plus 2 tbsp. butter, softened
¾ cups dark brown sugar
2 tsp. vanilla extract
4 extra-large eggs

For the chocolate fudge frosting:
1¼ cups superfine sugar
½ tsp. salt
4 oz. semisweet dark chocolate, chopped
1 cup milk
2 tbsp. light corn syrup
½ cup (1 stick) butter, diced
2 tsp. vanilla extract

1. Preheat the oven to 350°F. Lightly grease and line the bottoms of three 9-inch cake pans with wax paper or parchment paper. Sift the flour, baking soda, and salt into a bowl.

2. Sift the cocoa into another bowl and gradually beat in a little of the milk to form a paste. Continue beating in the milk until a smooth mixture results.

3. Beat the butter, sugar, and vanilla extract until light and fluffy, then gradually beat in the eggs, beating well after each addition. Stir in the flour and cocoa mixtures alternately in three or four batches.

4. Divide the mixture evenly among the three pans, smoothing the surfaces evenly. Bake in the preheated oven for 25-35 minutes until cooked and firm to the touch. Remove, cool, and turn out onto a wire rack. Discard the lining paper.

5. To make the frosting, put the sugar, salt, and chocolate into a heavy saucepan, and stir in the milk until blended. Add the light corn syrup and butter. Bring the mixture to a boil over medium-high heat, stirring to help dissolve the sugar.

6. Boil for 1 minute, stirring constantly. Remove from the heat, stir in the vanilla extract, and cool. When cool, beat until thickened and slightly lightened in color.

7. Sandwich the three cake layers together with about a third of the frosting, placing the third cake layer with the flat-side up.

8. Transfer the cake to a serving plate, and using a metal palette knife, spread the remaining frosting over the top and sides. Swirl the top to create a decorative effect, and serve.

# Chocolate & Coconut Cake

## Cuts into 8 slices

4 oz. semisweet dark
   chocolate, roughly chopped
¾ cup (1½ sticks) butter or
   margarine
⅔ superfine sugar
3 large eggs, beaten
1½ cups self-rising flour
1 tbsp. unsweetened cocoa
¾ cup unsweetened shredded
   dry coconut

For the frosting:
½ cup (1 stick) butter or
   margarine
2 tbsp. creamed coconut
2 cups confectioners' sugar
⅓ cup lightly toasted
   unsweetened shredded
   dry coconut

1. Preheat the oven to 350°F. Melt the chocolate in a bowl placed over a saucepan of gently simmering water. Make sure that the bottom of the bowl does not touch the water. When the chocolate has melted, stir until smooth and let cool.

2. Lightly grease and line the bottoms of two 7-inch layer cake pans. In a large bowl, beat the butter or margarine and sugar together until light and creamy. Beat in the eggs a little at a time, then stir in the melted chocolate.

3. Sift the flour and cocoa together and gently fold into the chocolate mixture with a metal spoon or rubber spatula. Add the shredded coconut and mix lightly. Divide between the two prepared pans and smooth the tops.

4. Bake in the oven for 25–30 minutes until a toothpick comes out clean when inserted into the center of the cake. Let cool in the pan for 5 minutes, then turn out, discard the paper, and leave on a wire rack until cool.

5. Beat together the butter or margarine and creamed coconut until fluffy. Add the confectioners' sugar and mix well. Spread half of the frosting on one layer and press the cakes together. Spread the remaining frosting over the top, sprinkle with the shredded coconut, and serve.

# Chocolate Buttermilk Cake

### Cuts into 8–10 slices

¾ cup (1½ sticks) butter
1 tsp. vanilla extract
1½ cups superfine sugar
4 large eggs, separated
¾ cup self-rising flour
¼ cup unsweetened cocoa
¼ cup buttermilk
7 oz. semisweet dark chocolate
7 tbsp. butter
1 cup heavy cream

1. Preheat the oven to 350°F. Lightly grease and line a deep 9-inch round cake pan. Cream together the butter, vanilla extract, and sugar until light and fluffy, then beat in the egg yolks, one at a time.

2. Sift together the flour and cocoa and fold into the egg mixture together with the buttermilk. Beat the egg whites until soft peaks form, and fold carefully into the chocolate mixture in two batches. Spoon the batter into the prepared pan, and bake in the preheated oven for 1 hour or until firm. Cool slightly, then turn out onto a wire rack and leave until completely cooled.

3. Place the chocolate and butter together in a heatproof bowl set over a saucepan of simmering water, and heat until melted. Stir until smooth, then leave at room temperature until the chocolate is thick enough to spread.

4. Split the cake horizontally in half. Use some of the chocolate mixture to sandwich the two halves together. Spread and decorate the top of the cake with the remaining chocolate mixture. Finally, whip the cream until soft peaks form and use to spread around the sides of the cake. Chill in the refrigerator until required. Serve cut into slices. Store in the refrigerator.

# Chocolate Brazil Nut & Polenta Squares

## Cuts into 9 squares

1¼ cups shelled Brazil nuts
⅔ cup (1¼ sticks) butter, softened
⅔ cup firmly packed golden brown sugar
2 large eggs, lightly beaten
¾ cup all-purpose flour
¼ cup unsweetened cocoa
¼ tsp. ground cinnamon
1 tsp. baking powder
pinch salt
⅓ cup milk
⅓ cup instant polenta

1. Preheat the oven to 350°F. Grease and line a deep 7-inch square pan with nonstick parchment paper. Finely chop ½ cup of the Brazil nuts and set aside. Coarsely chop the remainder. Cream the butter and sugar together until light and fluffy. Gradually add the eggs, beating well between each addition.

2. Sift the flour, unsweetened cocoa, cinnamon, baking powder, and salt into the creamed batter and then gently fold in using a large metal spoon or spatula. Add the milk, polenta, and ¾ cup of the coarsely chopped Brazil nuts. Fold into the batter.

3. Turn the batter into the prepared pan, leveling the surface with the back of the spoon. Sprinkle ½ cup of finely chopped Brazil nuts over the top. Bake the cake on the center shelf of the preheated oven for 45–50 minutes or until well risen and lightly browned, and when a clean toothpick inserted into the center of the cake for a few seconds comes out clean.

4. Leave the cake in the pan for 10 minutes to cool slightly, then turn out onto a wire rack to cool completely. Cut the cake into nine equal squares and serve. Store in an airtight container.

# Chocolate Walnut Squares

## Cuts into 24 squares

½ cup (1 stick) butter
5 oz. semisweet dark
   chocolate, broken
   into squares
2 cups superfine sugar
½ tsp. vanilla extract
1¼ cups all-purpose flour
¾ cup self-rising flour
½ cup unsweetened cocoa
1 cup mayonnaise, at room
   temperature

For the chocolate glaze:
4 oz. semisweet dark
   chocolate, broken
   into squares
3 tbsp. unsalted butter
24 walnut halves
1 tbsp. confectioners'
   sugar, for dusting

1. Preheat the oven to 325°F. Grease and line a 11 x 7 x 2 inch
   cake pan with nonstick parchment paper. Place the butter,
   chocolate, sugar, vanilla extract, and 1 cup cold water in a
   heavy saucepan. Heat gently, stirring occasionally, until the
   chocolate and butter have melted, but do not let boil.

2. Sift the flours and unsweetened cocoa into a large bowl, and
   make a well in the center. Add the mayonnaise and about one-
   third of the chocolate mixture, and beat until smooth.
   Gradually beat in the remaining chocolate mixture. Pour into
   the pan and bake in the oven for 1 hour or until slightly risen
   and firm to the touch. Place the pan on a wire rack and let
   cool. Remove the cake and peel off the paper.

3. To make the chocolate glaze, place the chocolate and butter in
   a small saucepan with 1 tablespoon of water, and heat very
   gently, stirring occasionally until melted and smooth. Let cool
   until the chocolate has thickened, then spread evenly over the
   cake. Chill the cake in the refrigerator for about 5 minutes,
   then mark into 24 squares.

4. Lightly dust the walnut halves with some confectioners' sugar,
   and place one on the top of each square. Cut into pieces and
   store in an airtight plastic container until ready to serve.

# Cranberry & White Chocolate Cake

## Cuts into 4 slices

**1 cup (2 sticks) butter, softened**
**1⅛ cup cream cheese**
**⅔ cup firmly packed golden brown sugar**
**1 cup superfine sugar**
**3 tsp. grated orange zest**
**1 tsp. vanilla extract**
**4 large eggs**
**3¼ cups all-purpose flour**
**2 tsp. baking powder**
**¾ cup cranberries, thawed if frozen**
**8 oz. white chocolate, coarsely chopped**
**2 tbsp. orange juice**

1. Preheat the oven to 350°F. Lightly grease and flour a 9-inch fancy tube mold (kugelhopf pan) or ring mold. Using an electric mixer, cream the butter and cheese with the sugars until light and fluffy. Add the grated orange zest and vanilla extract, and beat until smooth. Beat in the eggs, one at a time.

2. Sift the flour and baking powder together, and stir into the creamed batter, beating well after each addition. Fold in the cranberries and 6 oz. of the white chocolate. Spoon into the prepared mold and bake in the preheated oven for 1 hour or until firm and a toothpick inserted into the center comes out clean. Cool in the mold before turning out onto on a wire rack.

3. Melt the remaining white chocolate, stir until smooth, then stir in the orange juice and let cool until thickened. Transfer the cake to a serving plate and spoon over the white chocolate and orange glaze. Let set.

# Chocolate Box Cake

Cuts into 16 slices

1½ cups self-rising flour
1 tsp. baking powder
¼ cup superfine sugar
¼ cup butter, softened
3 extra-large eggs
3 tbsp. unsweetened cocoa

For the chocolate box:
10 oz. semisweet dark chocolate
½ cup apricot preserves

For the topping:
2 cups heavy cream
10 oz. semisweet dark
   chocolate, melted
2 tbsp. brandy
1 tsp. cocoa, to decorate

1. Preheat the oven to 350°F. Lightly grease and flour an 8-inch square cake pan. Sift the flour and baking powder into a large bowl, then stir in the sugar. Using an electric mixer, beat in the butter and eggs. Blend the cocoa with 1 tablespoon of water, then beat into the creamed mixture. Turn into the pan and bake in the oven for about 25 minutes or until well risen and cooked. Remove from the oven and cool before removing the cake from the pan.

2. For the chocolate box, break the chocolate into small pieces, place in a heatproof bowl over a saucepan of gently simmering water, and leave until soft. Stir it occasionally until melted and smooth. Line a jelly-roll pan with nonstick parchment paper, then pour in the melted chocolate, tilting the pan to level. Leave until set. Once set, turn out onto a chopping board and carefully strip off the paper. Cut into four strips, the same length as the cake, using a large, sharp knife that has been dipped into hot water. Gently heat the apricot preserves and strain to remove lumps. Brush over the top and sides of the cake. Carefully place the chocolate strips around the sides and press lightly. Let it set for at least 10 minutes.

3. For the topping, beat the cream to soft peaks, and quickly fold into the melted chocolate, along with the brandy. Spoon the chocolate cream into a pastry bag with a star tip and pipe rosettes over the surface. Dust with cocoa, and serve.

# Chocolate Chiffon Cake

## Cuts into 10–12 slices

½ cup unsweetened cocoa
2¾ cups self-rising flour
2½ cups superfine sugar
7 large eggs, separated
¼ cup vegetable oil
1 tsp. vanilla extract
¾ cup walnuts
7 oz. semisweet dark
  chocolate, melted

For the filling and glaze:
¾ cups (1½ sticks) butter
2½ cups confectioners'
  sugar, sifted
2 tbsp. unsweetened
  cocoa, sifted
2 tbsp. brandy

1. Preheat the oven to 325°F. Lightly grease and line a 9-inch round cake pan. Lightly grease a baking pan. Blend the unsweetened cocoa with ¾ cup of boiling water, and let cool. Place the flour and 1½ cups of the sugar in a large bowl, and add the cocoa mixture, egg yolks, oil, and vanilla extract. Beat until smooth and lighter in color. Beat the egg whites in a clean, grease-free bowl until soft peaks form, then fold into the cocoa mixture. Pour into the pan and bake in the oven for 1 hour or until firm. Leave for 5 minutes before turning out onto a wire rack to cool.

2. For the filling, cream together 1 stick of the butter with the confectioners' sugar, unsweetened cocoa, and brandy until smooth. Set aside. Melt the remaining butter and blend with about two-thirds of the melted semisweet dark chocolate. Stir until smooth and then leave until thickened. Place the rest of the sugar into a small, heavy saucepan over a low heat and heat until the sugar has melted and is a deep golden brown.

3. Add the walnuts and the remaining melted chocolate to the melted sugar and pour onto the baking pan. Leave until cold and brittle, then chop finely. Set aside. Split the cake into three layers, place one layer onto a plate, and spread with half of the frosting. Top with a second cake layer, spread with the remaining frosting, and arrange the third cake layer on top. Cover the cake with the thickened chocolate glaze. Sprinkle with the walnut praline and serve.

# Everyday Cakes

# Maple, Pecan & Lemon Loaf

## Cuts into 12 slices

3 cups all-purpose flour
1 tsp. baking powder
¾ cup (1½ sticks) butter, cubed
6 tbsp. superfine sugar
1 cup pecans, coarsely chopped
3 large eggs
1 tbsp. milk
finely grated zest of 1 lemon
5 tbsp. maple syrup

For the icing:
½ cup confectioners' sugar
1 tbsp. lemon juice
¼ cup pecans, coarsely chopped

1. Preheat the oven to 325°F. Lightly grease and line the bottom of a 9 x 5 x 3-inch loaf pan with nonstick parchment paper.

2. Sift the flour and baking powder into a large bowl. Rub in the butter until the mixture resembles fine bread crumbs. Stir in the superfine sugar and pecans.

3. Beat the eggs together with the milk and lemon zest. Stir in the maple syrup. Add to the dry ingredients, and gently stir in until mixed thoroughly to make a soft dropping consistency.

4. Spoon the mixture into the prepared pan, and level the top with the back of a spoon. Bake on the center shelf of the preheated oven for 50–60 minutes or until the cake is well risen and lightly browned. If a toothpick inserted into the center comes out clean, the cake is ready.

5. Leave the cake in the pan for about 10 minutes, then turn out, and let cool on a wire rack. Carefully remove the lining paper.

6. Sift the confectioners' sugar into a small bowl and stir in the lemon juice to make a smooth icing.

7. Drizzle the icing over the top of the loaf, then sprinkle with the chopped pecans. Let the icing set, slice thickly, and serve.

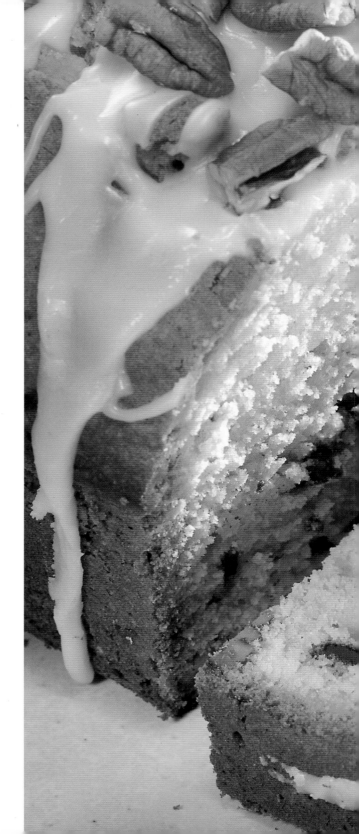

# Fat-Free Sponge

## Cuts into 8 slices

3 large eggs
heaping ¾ cup superfine
  sugar, plus extra for dusting
1 cup self-rising flour,
  plus extra for dusting

**To decorate:**
⅔ cup low-fat whipping cream, or low-fat
  crème fraîche or yogurt
2 tbsp. lemon curd
1 scant cup blueberries
zest of 1 lemon, cut into long
  thin strips

1. Preheat the oven to 375°F. Grease two nonstick 7-inch layer
   cake pans, line with nonstick parchment paper, then dust
   with a mixture of superfine sugar and flour.

2. Put the eggs and sugar in a large bowl and stand this over a
   pan of hot water. Beat the eggs and sugar until doubled in
   volume and the mixture is thick enough to leave a trail on
   the surface of the batter when the beaters are lifted away.

3. Remove the bowl from the heat and continue beating
   for another 5 minutes until the mixture is cool. Sift half
   the flour over the mixture and fold in very lightly, using
   a large metal spoon. Sift in the remaining flour and fold
   in the same way.

4. Pour the mixture into the prepared pans and tilt them
   to spread the mixture evenly. Bake for 15–20 minutes
   until well risen and firm and the cakes are beginning
   to shrink away from the sides of the pans. Let stand for
   2 minutes, then turn out to cool on a wire rack.

5. To decorate, whip the cream if using, and spread half the
   cream (or crème fraîche or yogurt) over one cake. Swirl
    tablespoon lemon curd into the cream, crème fraîche, or
   yogurt and scatter over half the blueberries. Place the other
   cake on top and swirl over the remaining cream/yogurt.
   Swirl over the remaining lemon curd and sprinkle with the
   remaining berries. Scatter the strips of lemon zest over the top.

# Lemony Coconut Cake

## Cuts into 10–12 slices

2½ cups all-purpose flour
2 tbsp. cornstarch
1 tbsp. baking powder
1 tsp. salt
⅔ cup (1¼ sticks) shortening or soft margarine
1¼ cups superfine sugar
grated zest of 2 lemons
1 tsp. vanilla extract
3 extra-large eggs
⅔ cup milk
4 tbsp. white rum
16-oz. jar lemon curd (available from specialty grocery stores)
lime zest, to decorate

For the frosting:
1¼ cups superfine sugar
½ cup water
1 tbsp. glucose
¼ tsp. salt
1 tsp. vanilla extract
3 extra-large egg whites
½ cup unsweetened shredded dry coconut

1. Preheat the oven to 350°F. Lightly grease and flour two 8-inch, round, nonstick cake pans.

2. Sift the flour, cornstarch, baking powder, and salt into a large bowl, and add the shortening or margarine, sugar, lemon zest, vanilla extract, eggs, and milk. With an electric mixer on a low speed, beat until blended, adding a little extra milk if the mixture is very stiff. Increase the speed to medium and beat for about 2 minutes.

3. Divide the mixture between the pans and smooth the tops evenly. Bake in the preheated oven for 20–25 minutes or until the cakes feel firm and are cooked. Remove from the oven, and cool before removing from the pans.

4. Put all the ingredients for the frosting, except the coconut, into a heatproof bowl placed over a saucepan of simmering water. Do not let the bottom of the bowl touch the water.

5. Using an electric mixer, blend the frosting ingredients on a low speed. Increase the speed to high, and beat for 7 minutes until the whites are stiff and glossy. Remove the bowl from the heat and continue beating until cool. Cover with plastic wrap.

6. Using a serrated knife, split the cake layers horizontally in half and sprinkle each cut surface with the white rum. Sandwich the cakes together with the lemon curd, and press lightly.

7. Spread the top and sides generously with the frosting, swirling the top. Sprinkle the coconut over the top and gently press onto the sides to cover. Decorate the coconut cake with the lime zest, and serve.

# Lemon Drizzle Cake

## Cuts into 16 squares

½ cup (1 stick) butter or margarine
¾ cup superfine sugar
2 extra-large eggs
1½ cups self-rising flour
2 lemons, preferably unwaxed
4 tbsp. granulated sugar

1. Preheat the oven to 350°F. Lightly grease and line the bottom of a 7-inch square cake pan with nonstick parchment paper.

2. In a large bowl, cream the butter or margarine and superfine sugar together until soft and fluffy. Beat the eggs, then gradually add a little of the egg to the creamed mixture, adding 1 tablespoon of flour after each addition.

3. Finely grate the zest from one of the lemons, and stir into the creamed mixture, beating well until smooth. Squeeze the juice from the lemon, strain, then stir into the mixture.

4. Spoon into the prepared pan, level the surface, and bake in the preheated oven for 25–30 minutes. Using a zester, remove the strips of zest from the remaining lemon, mix with 2 tablespoons of the granulated sugar, and set aside.

5. Squeeze the juice into a small saucepan. Add the rest of the granulated sugar to the lemon juice in the saucepan and heat gently, stirring occasionally. When sugar has dissolved, simmer gently for 3–4 minutes until syrupy.

6. With a toothpick or fine toothpick, prick the cake all over.

7. Sprinkle the lemon zest and sugar over the top of the cake, drizzle over the syrup, and let it cool in the pan. Cut the cake into squares and serve.

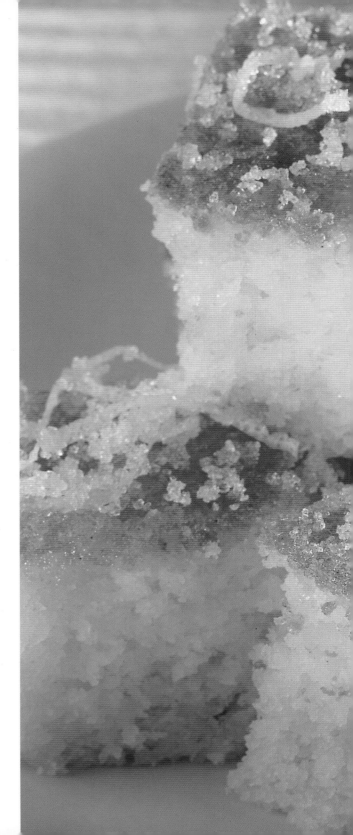

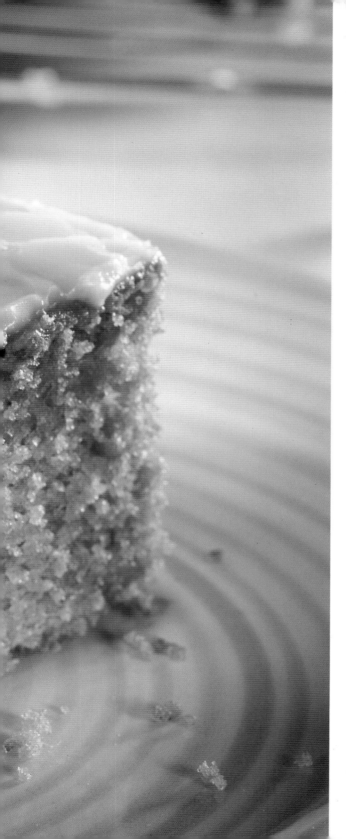

# Lemon-Iced Ginger Squares

## Cuts into 12 slices

**1 cup superfine sugar**
**4 tbsp. butter, melted**
**2 tbsp. molasses**
**2 large egg whites, lightly beaten**
**2 cups all-purpose flour**
**1 tsp. baking soda**
**½ tsp. ground cloves**
**1 tsp. ground cinnamon**
**¼ tsp. ground ginger**
**pinch salt**
**1 cup buttermilk**
**1 cup plus 4 tbsp. confectioners' sugar**
**lemon juice**

1. Preheat the oven to 400°F. Lightly grease an 8-inch square cake pan and sprinkle with a little flour.

2. Mix together the granulated sugar, butter, and molasses. Stir in the egg whites.

3. Mix together the flour, baking soda, cloves, cinnamon, ginger, and salt. Stir the flour mixture and buttermilk alternately into the butter mixture until well blended.

4. Spoon into the prepared pan and bake in the preheated oven for 35 minutes or until a toothpick inserted into the center of the cake comes out clean.

5. Remove from the oven and let cool for 5 minutes in the pan before turning out onto a wire rack over a large plate. Using a toothpick, make holes on the top of the cake.

6. Meanwhile, mix together the confectioners' sugar with enough lemon juice to make a smooth, pourable frosting.

7. Carefully pour the frosting over the hot cake, then leave until cool. Cut the ginger cake into squares, and serve.

# Easy Sponge Cake

## Cuts into 8 slices

1 cup soft margarine
heaping 1 cup superfine sugar
4 large eggs
1 tsp. vanilla extract
1 heaping cup
self-rising flour
1 tsp. baking powder
confectioners' sugar, to dust

For the filling:
4 tbsp. seedless raspberry jelly
scant ½ cup heavy cream

1. Preheat the oven to 350°F. Grease two 8-inch layer cake
   pans and line the bottoms with nonstick parchment paper.

2. Place the margarine, sugar, eggs, and vanilla extract in a large
   bowl and sift in the flour and baking powder. Beat for about
   2 minutes until smooth and blended, then divide between
   the pans and smooth level.

3. Bake for about 25 minutes until golden, well risen, and the
   tops of the cakes spring back when lightly touched with a
   fingertip. Let cool in the pans for 2 minutes, then turn out
   onto a wire rack to cool. When cool, peel away the
   parchment paper.

4. When completely cold, spread one cake with jelly and place
   on a serving plate. Whip the cream until it forms soft peaks,
   then spread on the underside of the other cake. Sandwich
   the two cakes together and sift a little confectioners' sugar
   over the top.

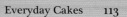

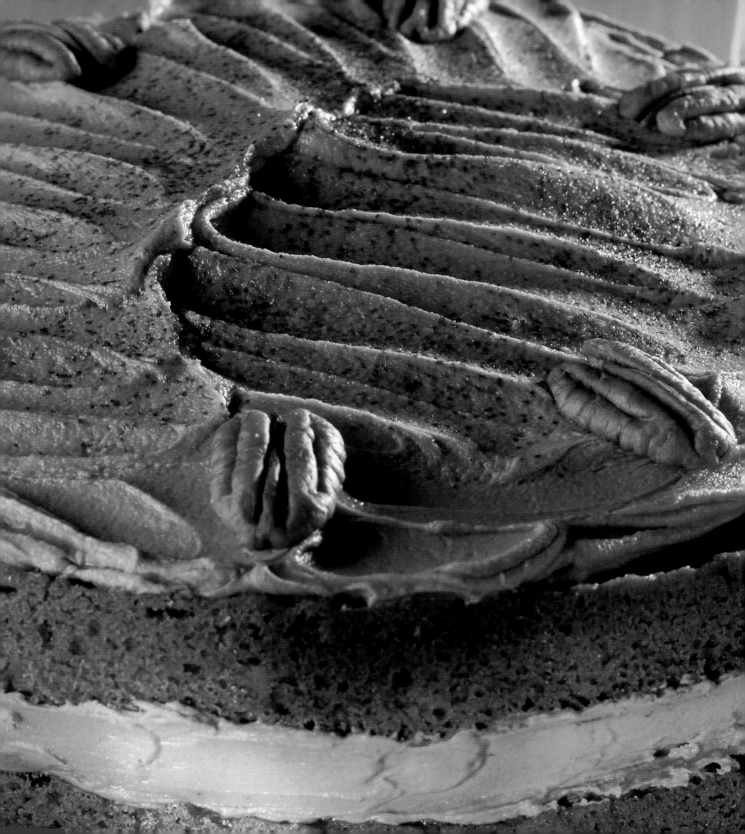

# Coffee & Pecan Cake

## Cuts into 8 slices

**1⅓ cups self-rising flour**
**½ cup (1 stick) butter**
  **or margarine**
**¾ cup brown sugar**
**1 tbsp. instant coffee**
**2 extra-large eggs**
**½ cup roughly**
  **chopped pecans**

**For the frosting:**
**1 tsp. instant coffee**
**1 tsp. unsweetened cocoa**
**6 tbsp. softened**
  **unsalted butter**
**1½ cups confectioners'**
  **sugar, sifted**
**whole pecans,**
  **to decorate**

1. Preheat the oven to 375°F. Lightly grease and line the bottoms of two 7-inch layer cake pans with wax paper or parchment paper. Sift the flour and set aside.

2. Beat the butter or margarine and sugar together until light and creamy. Dissolve the coffee in 2 tablespoons of hot water and let cool.

3. Lightly mix the eggs with the coffee liquid. Gradually beat into the creamed butter and sugar, adding a little of the sifted flour with each addition.

4. Fold in the pecans, then divide the mixture between the prepared pans, and bake in the preheated oven for 20–25 minutes or until well risen and firm to the touch. Leave in the pans for 5 minutes before turning out and cooling on a wire rack.

5. To make the frosting, blend the coffee and cocoa with enough boiling water to make a stiff paste. Beat into the butter and confectioners' sugar.

6. Sandwich the two cakes together using half of the frosting. Spread the remaining frosting over the top of the cake and decorate with the whole pecans to serve. Store in an airtight container.

# Citrus Cake

## Cuts into 6 slices

¼ cup brown sugar
¾ cup (1½ sticks) butter or margarine
3 large eggs
2 tbsp. orange juice
1½ cups self-rising flour
finely grated zest of 2 oranges
5 tbsp. lemon curd (available from specialty grocery stores)
1 scant cup confectioners' sugar
finely grated zest of 1 lemon
1 tbsp. freshly squeezed lemon juice

1. Preheat the oven to 375°F. Lightly grease and line the bottom
   of a round 8-inch cake pan with nonstick parchment paper.

2. In a large bowl, cream the sugar and butter or margarine
   together until light and fluffy. Beat the eggs together, and
   beat into the creamed mixture a little at a time.

3. Beat in the orange juice with 1 tablespoon of the flour. Sift
   the remaining flour onto a large plate several times, then with
   a metal spoon or rubber spatula, fold into the creamed
   mixture.

4. Spoon into the prepared cake pan. Stir the finely grated
   orange zest into the lemon curd, and dot randomly across the
   top of the mixture.

5. Using a fine toothpick, swirl the lemon curd through the
   cake mixture. Bake in the preheated oven for 35 minutes
   until risen and golden. Let cool for 5 minutes in the pan,
   then turn out carefully onto a wire rack.

6. Sift the confectioners' sugar into a bowl, add the grated
   lemon zest and juice, and stir well to mix. When the cake is
   cool, cover the top with the icing, and serve.

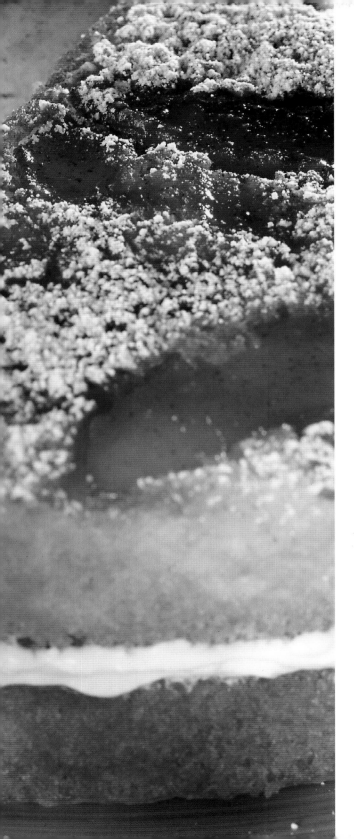

# Toffee Apple Cake

Cuts into 8 slices

**2 small apples, peeled**
**4 tbsp. dark brown sugar**
**¾ cup (1½ sticks) butter or margarine**
**¾ cup superfine sugar**
**3 large eggs**
**1½ cups self-rising flour**
**⅔ cup heavy cream**
**2 tbsp. confectioners' sugar**
**½ tsp. vanilla extract**
**½ tsp. ground cinnamon**

1. Preheat the oven to 350°F. Lightly grease and line the bottoms of two 8-inch layer cake pans with nonstick parchment paper.

2. Thinly slice the apples and toss in the brown sugar until well coated. Arrange them over the bottom of the prepared pans, and set aside.

3. Cream together the butter or margarine and superfine sugar until light and fluffy. Beat the eggs together in a small bowl, and gradually beat them into the creamed mixture, beating well between each addition.

4. Sift the flour into the mixture and, using a metal spoon or rubber spatula, fold in. Divide the mixture between the two cake pans and level the surface.

5. Bake in the preheated oven for 25–30 minutes until golden and well risen. Leave in the pans to cool.

6. Lightly whip the cream with 1 tablespoon of the confectioners' sugar and the vanilla extract.

7. Sandwich the cakes together with the cream. Mix the rest of the sugar and ground cinnamon together, sprinkle over the top of the cake, and serve.

# Honey Cake

## Cuts into 6 slices

**4 tbsp. butter**
**2 tbsp. superfine sugar**
**⅓ cup honey**
**1½ cups all-purpose flour**
**½ tsp. baking soda**
**½ tsp. pumpkin pie spice**
**1 large egg**
**2 tbsp. milk**
**¼ cup slivered almonds**
**1 tbsp. honey, to drizzle**

1. Preheat the oven to 350°F. Lightly grease and line the bottom of a 7-inch round cake pan with lightly greased parchment paper.

2. In a saucepan, gently heat the butter, sugar, and honey until the butter has just melted.

3. Sift the flour, baking soda, and pumpkin pie spice together into a bowl. Beat the egg and the milk until mixed thoroughly.

4. Make a well in the center of the sifted flour and pour in the melted butter and honey.

5. Using a wooden spoon, beat well, gradually drawing in the flour from the sides of the bowl. When all the flour has been beaten in, add the egg mixture, and mix thoroughly. Pour into the prepared pan and sprinkle with the slivered almonds.

6. Bake in the preheated oven for 30–35 minutes or until well risen and golden brown, and a toothpick inserted into the center of the cake comes out clean.

7. Remove from the oven, cool for a few minutes in the pan, turn out, and let cool on a wire rack. Drizzle with the remaining tablespoon of honey, and serve.

# Toffee Walnut Roll

## Cuts into 10–12 slices

| | |
|---|---|
| 4 extra-large eggs, separated | For the toffee walnut filling: |
| ½ tsp. cream of tartar | 2 tbsp. all-purpose flour |
| 1 cup confectioners' sugar, plus extra to dust | ⅔ cup milk |
| ½ tsp. vanilla extract | 5 tbsp. light corn syrup or maple syrup |
| 1 cup self-rising flour | 2 extra-large egg yolks, beaten |
| | ¼ cup toasted and chopped walnuts or pecans |
| | 1¼ cups double cream, whipped |

1. Preheat the oven to 375°F. Lightly grease and line a jelly roll pan with parchment paper. Beat the egg whites and cream of tartar until softly peaking. Gradually beat in ½ cup of the sugar until stiff peaks form.

2. In another bowl, beat the egg yolks with the rest of the confectioners' sugar until thick. Beat in the extract. Gently fold in the flour and egg whites alternately, using a metal spoon or rubber spatula. Do not overmix. Spoon the batter into the pan and spread evenly. Bake for 12 minutes or until well risen and golden, and the cake springs back when pressed.

3. Place a clean dish towel on a work surface, and lay a piece of baking parchment about 13 inches long on the towel and dust with confectioners' sugar. As soon as the cake is cooked, turn out onto the paper. Peel off the lining paper and cut off the crisp edges of the cake. Starting at one narrow end, roll the cake with the paper and towel. Transfer the cake to a rack to cool.

4. For the filling, put the flour, milk, and syrup into a small saucepan and place over a gentle heat. Bring to a boil, beating until thick and smooth. Remove from the heat and slowly beat into the beaten egg yolks.

5. Pour the mixture back into the saucepan and cook over a low heat until it thickens and coats the back of a spoon. Strain the mixture into a bowl and stir in the chopped walnuts or pecans. Cool, stirring occasionally, then fold in half of the whipped cream.

6. Unroll the cooled cake and spread with the filling. Roll again, and decorate with the remaining cream. Sprinkle with the confectioners' sugar, and serve.

# Fruit Cake

## Cuts into 10 slices

**1 cup (2 sticks) butter or margarine**
**1 cup (scant) brown sugar**
**finely grated zest of 1 orange**
**1 tbsp. molasses**
**3 extra-large eggs, beaten**
**2 ½ cups all-purpose flour**
**¼ tsp. ground cinnamon**
**½ tsp. pumpkin pie spice**
**pinch freshly grated nutmeg**
**¼ tsp. baking soda**
**½ cup mixed candied peel**
**¼ cup candied cherries**
**⅔ cup raisins**
**⅔ cup golden raisins**
**⅔ cup chopped dried apricots**

1. Preheat the oven to 300°F. Lightly grease and line a 9-inch round cake pan with a double thickness of wax paper.

2. In a large bowl, cream together the butter or margarine, sugar, and orange zest until light and fluffy, then beat in the molasses. Beat in the eggs, a little at a time, beating well between each addition.

3. Set aside 1 tablespoon of the flour. Sift the remaining flour, the spices, and baking soda into the mixture.

4. Mix all the fruits and the remaining flour together, then stir into the cake mixture. Turn into the prepared pan and smooth the top, making a small hollow in the center of the cake mixture.

5. Bake in the oven for 1 hour, then reduce the heat to 275°F.

6. Bake for an additional 1½ hours or until cooked and a toothpick inserted into the center comes out clean. Let cool in the pan, then turn the cake out, and serve. Otherwise, when cool, store in an airtight container.

# Almond Cake

## Cuts into 8 slices

**1 cup (2 sticks) butter or margarine**
**1 cup superfine sugar**
**3 extra-large eggs**
**1 tsp. vanilla extract**
**1 tsp. almond extract**
**1 cup self-rising flour**
**1½ cups ground almonds**
**⅓ cup blanched whole almonds**
**1 square semisweet dark chocolate**

1. Preheat the oven to 300°F. Lightly grease and line the bottom of an 8-inch round cake pan with wax paper or parchment paper.

2. Cream together the butter or margarine and sugar with a wooden spoon until light and fluffy.

3. Beat the eggs and extracts together in a small bowl. Gradually add to the sugar and butter mixture, and mix well between each addition.

4. Sift the flour, and mix with the ground almonds. Beat into the egg mixture until mixed well and smooth. Pour into the prepared cake pan. Roughly chop the whole almonds, and sprinkle over cake before baking.

5. Bake in the preheated oven for 45 minutes or until golden and risen, and a toothpick inserted into the center of the cake comes out clean.

6. Remove from the pan and let cool on a wire rack. Melt the chocolate in a small bowl placed over a saucepan of gently simmering water, stirring until smooth and free of lumps.

7. Drizzle the melted chocolate over the cooled cake, and serve once the chocolate has set.

# Chestnut Cake

Cuts into 8–10 slices

¾ cup (1½ sticks) butter, softened
¾ cup sugar
9 oz. canned sweetened chestnut purée
3 large eggs, lightly beaten
1½ cups all-purpose flour
1 tsp. baking powder
pinch ground cloves
1 tsp. crushed fennel seeds
½ cup raisins
½ cup toasted pine nuts
¾ cup confectioners' sugar
5 tbsp. lemon juice
pared strips of lemon zest, to decorate

1. Preheat the oven to 300°F. Grease and line a 9-inch springform pan. Beat together the butter and sugar until light and fluffy. Add the chestnut purée and beat. Gradually add the eggs, beating after each addition. Sift in the flour with the baking powder and cloves. Add the fennel seeds and beat. The mixture should drop easily from a wooden spoon when tapped against the side of the bowl. If not, add some milk.

2. Beat in the raisins and pine nuts. Spoon the mixture into the prepared pan and smooth the top. Transfer to the center of the oven and cook in the preheated oven for 55–60 minutes or until a toothpick inserted in the center of the cake comes out clean. Remove from the oven and leave in the pan.

3. Meanwhile, mix together the confectioners' sugar and lemon juice in a small saucepan until smooth. Heat gently until hot but not boiling. Using a toothpick, poke holes all over the cake. Pour the hot syrup evenly on top, and let it soak into the cake. Decorate with pared strips of lemon and serve.

# Double Marble Cake

Cuts into 8–10 slices

3 oz. white chocolate
3 oz. semisweet dark
 chocolate
¾ cup sugar
¾ cup (1½ sticks) butter
4 large eggs, separated
1 cup all-purpose flour, sifted
¾ cup ground almonds

For the topping:
2 oz. white chocolate,
 chopped
3 oz. semisweet dark
 chocolate, chopped
¼ cup heavy cream
¾ cup (1½ sticks)
 unsalted butter

1. Preheat the oven to 350°F. Lightly grease and line the bottom of an 8-inch cake pan. Break the white and dark chocolate into small pieces, then place in two separate bowls placed over two saucepans of simmering water, ensuring that the bowls are not touching the water. Heat until melted.

2. In a large bowl, cream the sugar and butter together until light and fluffy. Beat in the egg yolks, one at a time, and add a spoonful of flour after each addition. Stir in the ground almonds. In another bowl beat the egg whites until stiff. Gently fold in the egg whites and the remaining sifted flour alternately into the almond mixture until all the flour and egg whites have been incorporated. Divide the batter among two bowls. Gently stir the white chocolate into one bowl, then add the semisweet dark chocolate to the other bowl.

3. Place alternating spoonfuls of the chocolate batters in the cake pan. Using a toothpick, swirl the batters together to get a marbled effect, then tap the pan on the work surface to level the batter. Bake in the preheated oven for 40 minutes or until cooked through. Let cool for 5 minutes in the pan, then turn out onto a wire rack to cool completely.

4. For the topping, melt half of the cream and butter with the dark chocolate and the other half with the white and stir both until smooth. Cool, whisk until thick and swirl both colours over the top of the cake to create a marbled effect.

# Almond Fruit Cake

**2¼ cups mixed dried fruit**
**½ cup ground almonds**
**finely grated zest and juice of 1 lemon**
**⅔ cup (1¼ sticks) butter, softened**
**¾ cup unbleached superfine sugar**
**3 large eggs, beaten**
**1 cup all-purpose flour**
**¼ cup whole blanched almonds**

1. Preheat the oven to 350°F. Grease and line the bottom of a 7-inch-deep round cake pan with nonstick parchment paper.

2. Place the dried fruit in a bowl and stir in the ground almonds to coat the dried fruit.

3. Grate the zest finely from the lemon into the bowl, then squeeze out 1 tablespoon of juice and add to the same bowl. In another bowl, beat the butter and sugar together until light and fluffy. Beat in the eggs a little at a time, adding 1 teaspoon of flour with each addition.

4. Sift in the remaining flour, then add the fruit-and-almond mixture. Fold together with a large metal spoon until smooth. Spoon the mixture into the pan and make a dip in the center with the back of a spoon. Arrange the almonds over the top in circles.

5. Bake for 1 hour, then reduce the heat to 300°F and bake for an additional hour, or until a toothpick inserted into the center comes out clean. Cool in the pan for 5 minutes, then turn out to cool on a wire rack.

# Buttery Passion Fruit Cake

## Cuts into 8–10 slices

**2 scant cups all-purpose flour**
**1 tsp. baking powder**
**¾ cup (1½ sticks) unsalted butter, softened**
**1 cup plus 2 tbsp. superfine sugar,**
  **plus 1 tsp. for sprinkling**
**grated zest of 1 orange**
**1 tsp. vanilla extract**
**3 large eggs, beaten**
**2 tbsp. milk**
**6 ripe passion fruit**
**5 tbsp. confectioners' sugar**

1. Preheat the oven to 350°F. Lightly grease and line the bottom of a 5 x 9-inch loaf pan with wax paper. Sift the flour and baking powder into a bowl, and set aside.

2. Beat the butter, sugar, orange zest, and vanilla extract until light and fluffy, then gradually beat in the eggs, 1 tablespoon at a time, beating well after each addition. If the mixture appears to curdle or separate, beat in a little of the flour mixture.

3. Fold in the flour mixture with the milk until just blended. Do not overmix. Spoon lightly into the pan and smooth the top evenly. Sprinkle lightly with the teaspoon of superfine sugar. Bake in the oven for 55 minutes or until well risen and golden brown. Remove and cool for 15–20 minutes. Turn the cake out of the pan and discard the lining paper.

4. Cut the passion fruit in half, and scoop out the pulp into a sieve set over a bowl. Press the juice through using a rubber spatula or wooden spoon. Stir in the confectioners' sugar and stir to dissolve, adding a little extra sugar if necessary.

5. Using a toothpick, pierce holes all over the cake. Spoon the passion fruit glaze over the cake and allow it to seep in. Gently invert the cake onto a wire rack, then turn right-side up. Dust with confectioners' sugar and cool completely. Serve cold.

# Luxury Carrot Cake

## Cuts into 12 slices

2½ cups all-purpose flour
2 tsp. baking powder
1 tsp. baking soda
1 tsp. salt
2 tsp. ground cinnamon
1 tsp. ground ginger
1 scant cup dark brown sugar
½ scant cup superfine sugar
4 extra-large eggs, beaten
1 cup plus 2 tbsp. sunflower oil
1 tbsp. vanilla extract
4 carrots, peeled and grated (about 1 lb.)
14 oz. canned crushed pineapple, well drained
1 cup toasted and chopped pecans or walnuts

For the frosting:
¾ cup cream cheese, softened
4 tbsp. butter, softened
1 tsp. vanilla extract
2 cups confectioners'
  sugar, sifted
1–2 tbsp. milk

1. Preheat the oven to 350°F. Lightly grease a 9-inch round baking pan. Line the bottom with nonstick parchment paper. Grease, then dust with flour.

2. Sift the first 6 ingredients into a large bowl, and stir in the sugars to blend. Make a well in the center. Beat the eggs, oil, and vanilla extract together, and pour into the well. Using an electric mixer, gradually beat, drawing in the flour mixture from the side until a smooth batter forms. Stir in the carrots, crushed pineapple, and chopped nuts until blended.

3. Pour into the prepared pan and smooth the surface evenly. Bake in the preheated oven for 50 minutes or until firm and a toothpick inserted into the center comes out clean. Remove from the oven and let cool before removing from the pan and discarding the lining paper.

4. For the frosting, beat the cream cheese, butter, and vanilla extract together until smooth, then gradually beat in the confectioners' sugar until the frosting is smooth. Add a little milk, if necessary. Spread the frosting over the top. Refrigerate for 1 hour to set the frosting, then cut into squares and serve.

# Butterscotch Loaf

Cuts into 8 slices

1 banana, peeled
½ cup soft margarine
⅔ cup superfine sugar
2 large eggs
1 tsp. almond extract
½ tsp. vanilla extract
1 cup self-rising flour
½ cup semisweet dark
  chocolate chips
⅔ cup chopped walnuts

**To decorate:**
heaping ⅓ cup confectioners' sugar
8 unbleached, natural rough-cut
  sugar cubes, chopped

1. Preheat the oven to 325°F. Grease and line the bottom of a
   9 x 5 x 3-inch loaf pan with a long thin strip of nonstick
   parchment paper.

2. Place the banana in a bowl and mash. Add the margarine,
   sugar, and eggs along with the extracts, and sift in the flour.
   Beat until smooth, then stir in the chocolate chips and add half
   the chopped walnuts. Stir until smooth, then spoon into the
   pan and spread level.

3. Bake for about 45 minutes until a toothpick inserted into the
   center comes out clean. Let stand in the pan for 5 minutes,
   then turn out to cool on a wire rack, peel away the paper and
   let stand to cool completely.

4. To decorate, make the confectioners' sugar into a runny
   consistency with 2 teaspoons water. Drizzle over the cake and
   sprinkle over the remaining walnuts and the chopped sugar
   cubes. Let stand for 30 minutes to set, then serve sliced.

# Banana Cake

Cuts into 8 slices

**3 ripe medium-size bananas**
**1 tsp. lemon juice**
**⅔ cup brown sugar**
**6 tbsp. butter or margarine**
**2¼ cups self-rising flour**
**1 tsp. ground cinnamon**
**3 large eggs**
**½ cup chopped walnuts**
**1 tsp. each ground cinnamon and superfine**
  **sugar, to decorate**
**heavy cream, to serve**

1. Preheat the oven to 375°F. Lightly grease and line the bottom of a 7-inch round cake pan.

2. Mash two of the bananas in a small bowl, sprinkle with the lemon juice and a heaping tablespoon of the sugar. Mix together lightly, and set aside.

3. Gently heat the remaining sugar and butter or margarine in a small saucepan until the butter has just melted. Pour into a small bowl, then let cool slightly. Sift the flour and cinnamon into a large bowl and make a well in the center.

4. Beat the eggs into the cooled sugar mixture, pour into the well of flour, and mix thoroughly. Gently stir in the mashed banana mixture. Pour half of the mixture into the prepared pan. Thinly slice the remaining banana, and arrange over the cake mixture.

5. Sprinkle over the chopped walnuts, then cover with the remaining cake mixture. Bake in the preheated oven for 50–55 minutes or until well risen and golden brown. Let cool in the pan, turn out, and sprinkle with the cinnamon and superfine sugar. Serve hot or cold with a pitcher of heavy cream for pouring.

# Marmalade Loaf Cake

## Cuts into 8–10 slices

¾ cup plus 2 tbsp. superfine sugar
¾ cup (1½ sticks) softened butter
3 large eggs, beaten
1⅓ cups self-rising flour
finely grated zest and juice
  of 1 orange
⅓ cup orange marmalade

**For the topping:**
zest and juice of 1 orange
1 cup confectioners' sugar

1. Preheat the oven to 350°F. Grease and line a 9 x 5 x 3-inch loaf pan with a long, thin strip of nonstick parchment paper.

2. Place the sugar and butter in a bowl and beat until light and fluffy. Add the beaten egg a little at a time, adding 1 teaspoon of flour with each addition.

3. Add the remaining flour to the bowl with the orange zest, 2 tablespoons orange juice, and the marmalade. Using a large metal spoon, fold the mixture together using a figure–eight movement until all the flour is incorporated. Spoon the batter into the pan and smooth level.

4. Bake for about 40 minutes until firm in the center and a toothpick inserted into the center comes out clean. Cool in the pan for 5 minutes, then turn out to cool completely on a wire rack.

5. To make the topping, peel thin strips of zest away from the orange and set aside. Squeeze the juice from the orange. Sift the confectioners' sugar into a bowl and mix with 1 tablespoon orange juice until a thin, smooth consistency forms. Drizzle over the top of the cake, letting it run down the sides. Scatter over the orange zest and let stand to set for 1 hour.

# Index